NL

LOOKING AT NORFOLK

Jane Hales & Wm. Bennett

LOOKING
AT NORFOLK

A sequel to 'The East Wind'
an unusual Guide to Norfolk

Illustrations by
FRANCIS KING

With Grateful Acknowledgements to
THE EASTERN COUNTIES NEWSPAPERS LTD.
"NORFOLK FAIR" AND THE "NORFOLK LIFE"

First published in book form
October 1971
Reprinted July 1972
Reprinted June 1988

Printed in Great Britain

To those who
like the look of Norfolk
and the tongue

Published by
Charles N. Veal & Company
PUBLISHERS
2 & 3 UNION PLACE • THE CRESCENT • WISBECH
CAMBRIDGESHIRE PE13 1HB

Contents

CONTENTS—continued

CONTENTS—continued

List of Illustrations

Section One

RIVERS AND ROADS

Ford over the River Glaven at Little Thornage

THE CHET

"THE CHET", wrote somebody, "is one of the least of the navigable rivers of Norfolk and Suffolk". It is indeed an unsung stream for three-quarters of its course, and that is only 12 miles long. The source is unremarked, near Poringland Fiveways, 4 miles from Norwich.

Poringland is a village hustled by the Norwich to Bungay road, but off it, in Carr's Lane, is Crome's Oak, said to be the original of the famous picture. It is in a suburban setting now, a captured denizen of a sweeter England.

Brooke is the next parish upon the Chet's modest course. Two hundred years ago it was described as a "handsome village, with some neat houses as summer retreats from Norwich". It is still neat, and three times winner of the county competition for the best kept village. Brooke church has the distinction of having celebrated the first harvest festival in Britain, last century.

Between Brooke and Bergh Apton church, a minor road passes over the Chet, a bloused-up stream, seeming hardly to move. Then it slinks through a wood, secretly, parallel to the road, and comes out on to a meadow overlooked by a thatched farmhouse.

So the Chet crosses the country to Chedgrave, which adjoins Loddon. Indeed "Loddon" is an old name for the stream. Up Loddon's narrow street chases the insistent traffic between Norwich and Lowestoft, under it creeps the Chet, and here is a mill whose wheels it once turned. The Chet looks a tired stream, as though it was finding its overgrown course too hard to fight against, but lower down, at the Staithe, it takes new life, and there are Broads boats sailing upon it.

Loddon has a market every other Monday, behind the Swan Inn, a high brick building with blue tiles. Almost opposite, set back in a great green graveyard, is the 15th-century church with the proud tower. Inside, it is very light, for there is no stained glass except for some shields in the east window.

Just south of Loddon, a small tributary joins the Chet, and it flows through the meadow and thicket of Hales Green. The Green has 66 acres, and it is rather difficult to get into for the tracks leading to it are narrow and muddy. The place itself resembles England of centuries ago. Here and there are steep-roofed houses all but hidden by tall orchard and other trees. Tragedies must have happened within them, though it seems strange that anything but content could be a sojourner.

Hales Hall on the Green is a mysterious place of fallen grandeur, of which very little seems to be known. There is a long brick building amongst barns and weeds. It is said to have been stables, and a group of four embossed Tudor chimneys show behind. Last century this place was a farmhouse ; a hundred years ago, at any rate, the foundations of the outer walls of the hall could still be traced, surrounded by a moat. It was founded by Sir James Hobart, Lord Chief Justice of the Court of Common Pleas, who died in 1525. "His benefactions and good works testify his charity and generosity." He built "the elegant parish church of the Holy Trinity at Loddon". Lady Dionis Williamson, a descendant, who lived at Hales Hall, gave £2000 towards the rebuilding of St. Paul's after the Fire of London.

Returning to the main course of the Chet, below Loddon, in 1884 it was "too narrow and insignificant for pleasure sailing", yet in the 'thirties of this century it was still used by big wherries. Then, in 1958, the 3 miles from the mouth to Loddon was dredged. In 1946, the Chet burst its banks and flooded 100 acres of marsh.

The final course of the Chet is through the parish of Hardley. "The church", wrote someone is 1828, "is a simple pile covered with lead, and a round tower", of which some reverend gentleman was curate for 65 years in the 18th century. It stands apart from the village which has a few scattered cottages, some of them very pleasant to look at, on the edge of the great green marshes of the Yare, and Chet. On the other side rises the bulk of Cantley sugar factory, and a woman from Hardley, who works there, goes across the marsh, and uses a rowing boat to get over the Yare.

Another mysterious house, Hardley Hall, is a short distance from the village street. *Kelly's Directory* pompously noted it as having been once "an important country seat". Backed by trees, overlooking the empty marsh, this Tudor house in its solitary setting, seems very serene. The stout walls are of flint, brick, and stone, the latter filched, maybe, from Langley Abbey, in the next village, after the Dissolution. It has an 18th-century wing, and from perhaps the middle of that period it was used as a farmhouse.

Between Hardley and Langley is the base of a 16th-century boundary cross. An old woman in red is said to sit on it of a night time. It is deep in nettles, so it cannot be a comfortable seat !

4

Hardley Cross, which is where the Chet joins the Yare, marked the limit of Jurisdiction of the City of Norwich over the main river ; lower down it belonged to Yarmouth. An inhabitant of Hardley was asked what the Cross was like, "Tell the truth", he replied, "I've lived here over sixty year, and I don't recollect, 'cause I haint been there only once."

THE GLAVEN

IT IS only a minor river. "Here is a small spring or head of a rivulet—a nameless thing indeed—unknown to geographers, unnoticed by historians—unsung by poets . . . running among the hills it is the boundary of divers parishes ; it produced fish, turns four corn mills, helping to prepare for man his daily bread, and after a very short course, falls into the sea at Cley." Thus it was described nearly 200 years ago, and it flows through what was termed the Garden of Norfolk. By car and by foot, it makes a pleasant day's excursion to follow its 8-10 mile course.

Long ago, the Glaven was known as the Hempstead Beck ; rumour says it starts from Hell Hole, a pit far away over the field, on the borders of Bodham and Beckham, but the pit proved to be dry, and clothed with elder and other scrub. But is seems to rise not far off, in a commonplace potato and sugar beet field, an insignificant ditch. This is certainly not the Garden of Norfolk. The water is hardly visible beneath nettles, loosetrife, and meadowsweet, and the ditch trails away down hill. But farther on there is water enough by the farmhouse to please the ducks and geese, and a brilliant cock and some hens pick delicately in a moist meadow.

There is another and more romantic source, a trickle from the moat of Baconsthorpe Old Hall (they call it Baconsthorpe Castle on the signposts). Some years ago, this was a wild and neglected place, with snowdrops growing here and there, straggling box edging in the old kitchen garden within the moat, and apple blossom in season. Now the ruin has been trimmed up by the Office of Works, and has smooth lawns.

The inner gatehouse is the most impressive part of the ruin. The outer gatehouse was occupied by a farmer and his family till 1920, when part of it fell down one winter night. The family of Heydon inhabited the main hall for about 200 years, and building was begun by Sir Henry Heydon at the end of the 15th century. He was an unscrupulous and unpleasant fellow, an enemy of the Pastons. His descendant, Sir Christopher, was more likeable, and a great flockmaster, who is said to have entertained thirty master shepherds one Christmas. The Heydons fought for the King in the Civil War, and impoverished themselves. The last one, who died in 1689, sold the Hall to a London woollen draper.

It is the Selbrigg Pond that is the main source of the Glaven. It was made as a decoy in the opening years of the last century. Nearby, the great Hempstead woods were felled in the last war, and replanted by the Forestry Commission with dark conifers. They stretch along the Glaven valley to the first mill by the Hempstead-Holt road. Below the mill, the stream flows through wet meadows, the boundary between Hempstead and Holt, to Smokers Hole, where there are the ruins of another very old mill house. In it lived Long Sall, all alone. She had to leave during the war because the explosions, made by soldiers on the adjoining common of Holt Lows, threatened to tumble down her house.

Farther on, the Glaven flows beneath the Holt-Edgefield road. Here is a tributary from Dam Hills, where once monks had a mill, and of recent years a decoy has been constructed on the site. The stream flows on through damp secluded lands towards Hunworth, and until not so long ago, the narrow road there had two fords, Sad to say, the authorities have bridged them. It was a Saturday afternoon, and several little boys were playing with the water near a ford. Suddenly a short, red-faced woman came round the corner, shouting at them. "You little warmints you, I know all yer names, and I won't have yer in this here meddar meddling with things." So the noisy battle continued, till the boys were routed, and the sound of the stream gurgling over the ford reasserted itself. The woman winked, belying her fierce demeanour. In her hand she had held a white hen's egg throughout the encounter. "That's like this here", she said, "them boys come inter the meddar a-fishin', and them jam jars for the little totty fish topple inter the stream, and the ol' cows jam on 'em and cut their feet."

The Glaven flows through Hunworth (locally called "Honey"). It is one of the most pleasant villages in Norfolk, but, alas, the old oaks on the hill above have been felled ! Hunworth and Stody adjoin ; there is a mill at Stody now disused. From Stody church on the hill comes another little stream to join the Glaven. In this delectable valley Chaucer walked (according to Walter Rye). Farther down, the Glaven flows through the silent mill at Thornage, and on to Little Thornage ford, where yellow mimulus grows.

At Letheringsett, the Stream is much in the public eye, for over it runs the A.148. Here is a round-towered church, and just within the graveyard gate is a tombstone bearing the inscription : "The Burial Place of Johnson Jex who died Jan. 5th, 1852, aged 73 years, born in obscurity, He passed his days at Letheringsett a Village Blacksmith. By the force

7

of an original and inventive genius Combined with indomitable perseverance, He mastered some of the greatest difficulties of Science : Advancing from the forge to the crucible. And from the horseshoe to the chronometer : Acquiring by mental labour a vast and varied amount of mechanical skill, and general knowledge. He was a man of scrupulous integrity, and moral worth, but, regardless of wealth, and insensible to the voice of fame, he lived and died a scientific anchorite." The Stream glides through two beautiful gardens, and enters Bayfield Park, where it broadens out into a small lake. Above it is the Hall and the ruins of a church ; on the opposite side of the valley is Summerhouse Hill, and Hull Wood, with the ancient oaks. The road, which must be one of the most beautiful in Norfolk, skirts the park, by the long flint wall. For many years, at Bayfield Hall, lived Sir Alfred Jodrell, that queer little man who has left such an impression on the immediate neighbourhood (he died in 1929). It was he who restored from a ruinous state, Glandford church, on the hillock above the ford, and rebuilt the village with substantial flint and brick cottages. He also put up the Shell Museum, which is worth a visit. Here, at Glandford, are, at last, signs of salt water, for there are dabs to be caught where the water gushes out from under the mill.

The high arched bridge called "Nowhere" spans the Glaven at Wiveton. In the sea flood of 1953 it *was* nowhere, being submerged, and the valley returned to its former state—an estuary of salt water. In former days, ships from the open sea sailed right up to Wiveton. In 1587 one was laden with oil, dried fat, and, to delight the children "Babies" (dolls) and "rattells" from Germany. In Charles II reign there was consternation when someone built a bank at Cley, preventing the passage of ships up to Wiveton. Later, it was demolished, but silting had increased. Eventually another bank was put up, at the beginning of the last century. Wiveton is permanently shut off from the sea except when a great surge breaks down man's puny barriers, and that only happens "once in a lifetime".

At last the Glaven flows through a sluice into the salt water channel of Cley, and so out to the waiting sea, by the ever increasing sands and shingles of Blakeney Point.

THE TAS

LESS than two centuries ago the citizens of Norwich had the best of two worlds : For the flourishing city ended at the Walls ; without was the fair countryside.

How different it is to-day ! A sprawl of houses engulfs even neighbouring villages—except to the south, where Lakenham ends abruptly at the River Tas, which after a 14-mile course, flows into the Yare at Trowse. On a hot summer day, children sport in the water, naiads in various degrees of nakedness.

Over the bridge the road runs straight to Caistor St. Edmunds, the Roman fortress of *Venta Icenorum*, with its grassy ditches and banks. Within the square enclosure were houses and public buildings ; there were stone ramparts, and a water-gate opening to the River Tas. The present church which stands inside the ditches contains stones from the old walls, and at one time, many cottages in the village showed Roman brick.

Farther up the Tas is Stoke Holy Cross. The mill is no longer working, but adjoining is a comfortable-looking house from which to look out upon the serene valley. In the church is a memorial to the Rev. Thomas Havers, who died in 1719. He was also a surgeon, and "cut for the stone", without, of course, anaesthetising his patients. "The instruments used in this fearful operation are faithfully represented on the monument".

At Shotesham All Saints is a sign declaring it to have been the best-kept village in Norfolk. It is certainly one of the most beautiful. Here are the typical plaster-and-thatch houses of South Norfolk, bright in the sun, with flowers before them, overlooking a little stream which feeds the Tas. In tangled meadows, horses flick their tails against the flies.

Shotesham Mill was pulled down years ago. Near where it stood, in a shady place, is a ford through the main course of the Tas, and a low glossy waterfall ; for there are still some fords across the river and its tributaries. How pleasant they are to pass through, yet the authorities seem to have a down on them.

There are two Shoteshams—All Saints and St. Mary's, the latter being sometimes called Little or Low Shotesham. At the Conquest there were four churches ; now, All Saints and

9

St. Mary's are still used, and near the latter is the ruined tower and an arch of St. Martin's, overhung with funeral ivy. St. Botolph's was pulled down after the Reformation and the graveyard ploughed up.

In the 18th century there was "a very agreeable Cold-Bath in the parish of St. Mary, filled up for the publick benefit at the expence of Will Fellowes Esq., who also founded the Norfolk and Norwich Hospital. His son, Robert, went in for politics instead of building". Parson Woodforde recorded in 1799, "There are two Candidates, a Mr. Freare, and a Mr. Fellowes of Shotesham. I hope the former will win as he is a Well Wisher to Government." For Woodforde was a Tory, and he got his wish, for Fellowes was beaten this time. There is still a Mr. Fellowes at Shotesham Park, through which flows the Tas, and the trees stand about slim and solemn.

Higher up the Tas, at Saxlingham Thorpe, the Norwich to Ipswich road intrudes upon the seclusion of the valley. Here are two bridges, old and new, and a mill which stands partly in Saxlingham and partly in Newton Flotman, with willows hanging over the water which give colour to the early spring. Newton Flotman is an interesting place name, for it was a settlement of the pirate Danes, "flotmann" means Dane.

* * * * *

At Tasburgh, which was another Roman station, two tributaries join the Tas. One from the east comes from beyond Hempnall, the parish to which so many signposts point. Here the little feeder of the Tas is a choked stream running under the street, and overhung with tea roses. This is a pleasant lively village ; by a high wall hollyhocks stretch themselves upwards. "Hempnall contains nothing remarkable", wrote a visitor in 1818. But during the Commonwealth the Rector got himself sequestrated for "observing the orders of the Church, declaring against Parliament and rebellion, opposing the lectures of godly ministers, and swearing by his faith and troth".

The other Tas tributary rises to the north-west, near Hethel, and not far away from Stanfield Hall, where the notorious Rush murder took place in 1848. The house is castellated, and stands within a moat, in a park studded with oak trees. On a November night, Rush shot dead Mr. Isaac Jermy and his son, and wounded Mrs. Jermy and a maid servant. Isaac Jermy was Recorder of Norwich at the time, and had had a dispute with Rush over the lease of a farm at Ketteringham. Rush was hanged on Norwich Hill the following April. Thousands witnessed his execution ; some had come by the new railway line to Norwich. "The greatest silence prevailed, the solemn stillness being only broken by the solitary shriek of a woman who had fainted in the crowd."

The main stream of the Tas rises between Tibenham and New Buckenham. In a ditch was a lusty growth of young nettles and water trickled through the back garden of a cottage, where nobody was at home. "They've gone out", said a man on the road, "do you want 'em ? "

"No, I'm looking for the rise of the Tas."

"They are out I say."

"Do you know where the Tas rises ? "

"Never heard tell of it", he said.

THE WENSUM
(Parson Woodforde's River)

THE Wensum joins the Yare at Trowse Eye, and there it loses its identity. It has not always suffered this indignity, for in Mary's reign a charter gave Norwich Corporation jurisdiction from Hellesdon Mill to Hardley Cross, 10 miles below, "on the river Wensum". At Trowse is a flint-and-brick cottage in a grassy place near the river, but beyond it looms up the power station and the dark shape of Norwich, a curious juxtaposition of rural and urban scenery. So up to Pull's Ferry, and the ancient water-gate to a creek which once penetrated to near the cathedral. In the early part of last century, a barge load of musicians floated along the river on Thursday afternoons, playing upon wind instruments, a "source of much gratification to attendant parties, who followed in other boats". Thirty years ago, a boat could be hired at the Ferry to penetrate the dark centre of Norwich. The water was shot with colours from urban waste ; it was a windy day, and a man on a bridge lost his hat into the water. The girl who was rowing took her hand from an oar to pick up the hat, but there was a heavy passenger in the stern, and the boat swung round. Again and again, the attempt was made with the same result, whilst the people on the bridge shouted mockingly.

The Back River, as the Wensum is called from the Dolphin Inn to Hellesdon Mill, was a favourite haunt of boating parties, but at the Mill boats had to be pulled over a ramp, and popped in on the other side. Now, up stream to a stretch of the Wensum which someone described thus in 1780. "The winding river through the villages . . . is uncommonly beautiful, and affords a scene, or to make use of a more fashionable word, a capability, for the highest improvements. The hills on each side of the river have been ornamented with plantations, and the stream glides gently on through the meadows below, giving a most romantic prospect of the country around." It is the same to-day.

Hereabouts is Parson Woodforde's country. He was not the kind of man to haunt anywhere, but with him we "enter into that country peace that is for ever England". At Ringland Brakes he went coursing hares ; he took a walk to Attlebridge with his brother, and was much fatigued. Higher up the stream, at Morton, one Burrows had stolen

12

Squire Custance's poultry to the value of 2 or 3 pounds. Upon his first coming to Weston Longville in May 1775, Woodforde found nothing to eat at the Rectory, so he had to dine at the Inn at Lenwade Bridge. Here too, he caught the Norwich chaise, and he went netting fish. "We caught at one draught two pails of Fish, Pike, Trout, and flat-fish. Prodigious sport indeed." In his time, the ruffe was popular eating, though nobody bothers about sampling these small fish to-day. "The body of this fish is all over rough, with sharp prickles and prickly fins. When the fish is angry, the fins stand up stiff, and flat again when the anger is over. The flesh of it is very wholesome and eats tender and short . . . much like the perch."

At Lyng, the Parson went fishing for Jacks (small pike) and he visited the paper mill, "the whole Machinery which is indeed very curious". He bought 10 quires of writing paper for 5s. The Mill works no longer, but the water surges through the arches of the old brick bridge. Two centuries ago, someone wrote, "The river enlarges itself in a beautiful meandering stream, pursues its course through meadows." To-day, on a hill at Lyng, above the valley, motor bicycles roar in "a scamble" ; Woodforde might have called the races "Tolerable Sport for young Persons."

On to Elsing Mill, which only stopped working in 1967. It is a white mill, there are swans in the stream, and guinea fowl and black sheep in a meadow. Higher up, the river skirts Bylaugh Park, where lived a friend of the Parson's. "Mr. Lloyd is a very agreeable Man, sings exceedingly well, keeps a Pack of Hounds, is a Captain in the Militia, a Justice of the Peace, and of Good Fortunes." After Mr. Lloyd's time, another house was built in the Park, begun in 1849. It was made of limestone blocks, and looked like an Italian palace, but, strangely enough, it did not jar with its Norfolk surroundings. A curse is said to have been on the new Hall, that it would not last a hundred years ; this was fulfilled, for it was demolished in the early 'fifties of this century. Now, saplings grow between roofless walls. The Church at Bylaugh is small, with a round tower, and queer hexagonal belfry. It stands on a smooth mound where snowdrops grow, and the Wensum glides by. Inside, is a double-decker pulpit, and box pews.

In Swanton Morley, at Castle Farm, by the Wensum, are morsels of Morley Castle, which turn up in an elder thicket. Sir Robert de Morley, "admiral of the king's fleet", gained such a notable victory near Sluse in Flanders that "the like sea-fight was never before seen ; he was also in the glorious battle of Crécy in France, Constable of the Tower of London . . ." The present occupants of Castle Farm seem

13

to have the best of both worlds. In this safe and solitary retreat, children and dogs can roam as they choose, freed from the menace of traffic, whilst their elders are able to reach the urban precincts of Dereham in a few minutes by motor car.

Higher up still, on the opposite side of the Wensum to Castle Farm, are the flint and carrstone remains of a Saxon cathedral, for here, at North Elmham, was a bishopric before there was one at Norwich. "My nephew took a ride this morning to Elmham to see an ancient Roman Lamp lately dug up there", wrote Woodforde. "He drew a sketch of it on paper with his Pencil." Above the river, beyond Elmham, was County School. The great house was built for a new public school, and the foundation stone was laid by the Prince of Wales, afterwards Edward VII, in 1873, but the school only lasted for twenty years. Afterwards, the house became Watts Naval Training School. It was demolished in recent years.

At Guist, the Wensum is spanned by a bridge (1931) but nearby is the old humped-back toll bridge, built by William Norris in 1773, and the chain, marking the old ford beside it, is still there. The son of the last gate-keeper lives in the house, and remembers the charge of 1d. per wheel levied on passing vehicles. The heir of the last Squire Norris fell in the Great War, and afterwards the estate was sold. The river wanders on through the marshy valley below Sennowe Park, by Ryburgh it goes, between Fakenham and Hempton Green to Shereford, Doughton, and Tatterford ; near Tattersett, it is joined by the Tat, from Wicken Pool in Syderstone.

Many years ago there was an animated correspondence in the press regarding the true source of the Wensum. Some-one was sure it was at Whissonsett, somebody else near a wild rose bush within the parish of Colkirk, but the official source is at West Rudham. "They reckon that's over there among the willers", said a man who was cutting down a thorn tree. Over the pasture, just beyond the hedge, amid swampy ground and some sad willows, there was quite a watery ditch, where two birds were scavengering. So this was the rise of the 30-mile long Wensum.

14

THE YARE

The Yare causes more commotion than any other Norfolk river, except the Ouse, far away in the west. It rises within the parish of Shipdham, but the River Board ignores it till it reaches Garveston, where it flows under the road from a corridor of thicket, a small active stream. Garveston used to be pronounced "Garston", but now this seems to have gone out of fashion.

Lower down, at Hardingham, men were mending the bridge. "Is this the Yare?" The foreman was uncertain, but there was some excuse as the Blackwater is a tributary hereabouts. On to Runhall and Coston (formerly called "Cosson") where a bridge marks the boundary between the two parishes, and the stream makes a little waterfall beneath it. Coston is a small place of under twenty souls, with a miniature church, a mid-Victorian rectory, and a farmhouse. Beyond the grass by the stream is a thatched cottage, a brick pillar-box, bearing the capitals E.R., and a side road ending in a field. But Coston has had notable inhabitants; for the best part of three centuries, the Archdeacon of Norfolk had a country seat here, "Being a good house and six acres of land". He also served the church at Coston.

The Yare flows on its eastern course through a pleasant quiet valley, and the villages are away from the horrors and hustle of busy roads. The Mill at Marlingford is silenced, but for the passage of water; Parson Woodforde wrote, "Ben sold my wheat to the Marlingford Miller . . . to be carried thither next week". On the other side of the valley is Barford, where the Tiffy, which comes from beyond Wymondham, joins the Yare.

Farther downstream there is a mill at Bawburgh. The water surfs out of it, and this is a village which sticks in the memory. But it is no longer a centre of general attraction as it was in medieval times, when pilgrims "from all parts of the world visited St. Walstan's shrine, verily priests and people grew exceedingly rich . . . but when pilgrimages ceased, all such relics were abolished, the inhabitants came immediately to great poverty, and so continued till the church became so ruinous that it was scarce fit for divine service, and remained forsaken till 1633, when it was repaired". This little building with its round extinguisher-topped tower,

15

stands high. Below it, in a "holl", is a farmhouse, and in the ragged orchard behind is St. Walstan's Well, walled round about. Once people drank the water, but now this practise has ceased, for, likely enough, the farmyard drains into it. Bottles of water were fetched for ailing stock, and, maybe, still are. Two centuries ago, someone wrote of St. Walstan, "who being neither Monk nor Priest vowed (they say) to live chaste without a wife, and performed his promise by fasting on Fridays and Saints Vigils without any other grace. He died on the 3rd January, 1016, and became the God of the Fields in Norfolk."

By the bequest of John Wagstaffe, a verse writer, if two natives of Bawburgh marry and have a child within two years, the fortunate infant is to receive a silver spoon. Nowadays the rules are seldom satisfied, and a spoon has not been awarded for about a decade.

Below Bawburgh, the Yare skirts Norwich, through Bowthorpe, Colney, and under the Wymondham road at Cringleford. A mill was here at Domesday, but the last one was burnt down in 1916. The house remains ; a century ago there were white water lilies in the river, but the last disappeared a dozen years ago.

The Wensum joins the Yare at Trowse, and somebody called the lower course "a river of commerce rather than an inspiration for romance and charming waltzes". Nevertheless, Whitlingham Reach seemed a veritable paradise after the war, when people had time to lie on the grass under trees, and frolic in boats. Somebody wrote about a century ago of the ruined church of Whitlingham. "The whole stands on the edge of a tremendous precipice . . . the grounds round the church are very picturesque, and invite the pen of the artist". The man on the high road had worked in the fields near the ruin. "Whether that's there still I can't say," he said. But there it was, ivy-clad, on top of a very steep bank. Nettles and elders—those slum-trees of the woods—cascaded down into the dell. The White House was not far away. Once it was an inn "much resorted to in the summer season by the holiday folks of Norwich on account of the scenery . . . A spot remarkable for a singular echo."

Below Whitlingham, on the south side of the Yare, is Surlingham, but the ferry boat was made away with during the 1939-45 war. Opposite is the parish of Postwick, and a large sea-going ship was trying to turn a corner of the river, looking as though it was wedged from bank to bank. Surlingham Broad, at the end of its dyke, is much overgrown, and a spawning place for roach and bream. Viewed by moonlight, a spectator declared it "reminded him of a Stilton cheese all alive with maggots". Farther down still is

Rockland Broad, and Buckenham Ferry, which is no longer working.

At the edge of Hassingham woods, to the north of the river, is the small two-tiered thatched church with its round tower, the roof of which was destroyed by fire in 1970. Nearby is the comforting sight of a white house, the reed-woven roof latticed by leafing boughs. Beyond the damp jungle of trees is the marsh where "a man may wander all day and hear no voices except those of the sedge warblers, larks, and meadow pipits".

The Yare, in its wide valley, splits the country in two, there being no public means of crossing between Norwich and Reedham Ferry, 20 miles or so apart. The scene is dominated by the high white towers of Cantley sugar factory. At Reedham is the New Cut which connects the Yare with the Waveney and the sea at Lowestoft. This was completed in 1833, and the first two ships to make the passage were towed from Surlingham to Norwich by a steam tug, a band playing, and flags flying. But the dreams of the promoters of making Norwich an important port were never fully realised, nor were the Yarmouth people, at the true mouth of the Yare, ruined, as was their fear.

THE NORWICH TO HOLT ROAD

WHEN Thomas Moore, farmer of Warham, noted in his diary for 1805 that he passed through St. Augustine's Gates, Norwich, he must have been writing from old custom, for the Gates had been demolished eleven years before. Anyhow, he rode his chestnut mare through the line of the walls, and north towards the Holt road. "Wind north east with snow and sleet", and he had a 30-odd mile journey home. Even in the early 'sixties of the last century there were only a few odd houses between the walls and Mile Cross.

Four miles farther on, Horsford had a population of about 500 when Moore went through it, but the portly oak by the stream looked much the same as it does to-day. About 120 years later somebody, emulating the old manner, walked the long road from Holt to Norwich. Very tired and footsore she stopped at Horsford "Dog" for a glass of cider, and learnt there a piece of scandal about Holt unknown to her ! Of recent times new houses have sprawled about Horsford, but there are two flint cottages bearing the dates 1837 and 183- on the fronts in large bottle-end figures. The incomplete inscription is due to a new addition of brickwork. Nearby, is the inn (closed recently) called the "Flagcutters", but familiarly the "Furrer Chucks", for once peat was cut on Horsford heath. There were plenty of poachers, and people felled small trees upon the waste. Two centuries ago, the Holt road ran for miles across heathland, and some remains, though here and there it is separated from the road by fields.

Farther on, at Haveringland, is the "Colt Blow" (Marsham Arms) a nice plain building but now disfigured by a modern porch. This is about a third of the distance from Holt—a fact well appreciated by travellers who walked or went on foot. Between here and Corpusty there are long stretches of straight road, not so pleasant as they used to be when one passed through a funnel of trees, but some haggard oaks still remain, struggling in a Philistine world, to perpetuate the goodness of old England. How testing must these straight roads have been to the pedestrian ! Yet tough men walked from Holt to Norwich, played cricket, and returned on foot.

Cawston "Woodrow" used to be the halfway stop on the journey. The sign was slung across the road, a welcome

18

sight to travellers needing food and drink. The light of a window showed far away to the south. Now, alas, the sign has gone, and the old house adjoins a garage. The "Woodrow", about 14 miles inland, is a landmark of climate. On a warm summer day, a cooler breeze is perceptible here to the traveller from Norwich to Holt. How often, in winter, there will be snow as far as the "Woodrow", and clear roads beyond, or contrariwise !

Near here is a row of trees which contain the Duel Stone. It marks a duel of 1698, when Sir Henry Hobart of Blickling fought Oliver Le Neve of Witchingham. It was Sir Henry who picked the quarrel, probably because he was in a bad mind at losing his seat in Parliament, but he suffered for it, for Le Neve ran him through the belly with a fatal wound. The victor fled to Holland on a "terribly windy Saturday", where he had to stay for more than a year.

A few miles north of the "Woodrow", the road runs parallel with the defunct Melton Constable-Yarmouth railway line. In the old days, the single cylinder De Dion Bouton had little chance of winning the race with a train, for its maximum speed was 25-30 miles an hour. Bluestone Halt, now a dwelling-house, can be seen through the trees. The Halt got the name of Bluestone from the number of blue stones ploughed up hereabouts.

Corpusty Church, solitary, serene, deserted, stands above the valley of the upper Bure, roughly two-thirds of the distance to Holt. One day in the last century, Clement Hardy, of Cley Hall, was driving his horse home from Norwich when he overtook his friend Bob. He went down the hill to the adjoining villages of Corpusty and Saxthorpe, and a mile beyond the latter he overtook Bob again. Clement was amazed at this occurrence, for he did not know of the very narrow road leading off to the left, near the top of Corpusty hill, passing through Little London, and rejoining the main road on the other side of Saxthorpe. This was the quickest route for the horse, or even the early motor car, for the ford at Saxthorpe was so deep that a horse was kept handy to pull out stranded mechanical vehicles. A bridge was built after the 1912 August flood ; the mill hard by is a pleasant blue-and-white building, with a tall angelica growing in a corner.

Edgefield is the last village on the Holt road. Here is a Green, and near it is an inn commonly called the "Pigs" (Bacon Arms). It is a scattered parish, and in the 'eighties Parson Marcon moved the church from below the Mount (where there was a beacon) to a more central place, but the tower of the old building still stands. From Edgefield opens up a wide view of the heath and woods of the Holt shelf.

19

Edgefield Old Church Tower

The road passes Potter's Farm, mellow and L-shaped. Tom Potter had a white beard and wore corduroys ; he remembered the year when his harvestmen forsook the scythe for the first mechanical reaper. He died in 1918 aged 96, and the year before he went out with a shooting party.

Half a mile farther on is the hill down to the sweet Glaven valley. On the right is a decoy made in recent times, but the field name is Dam Hills, and here was a medieval water mill. On the opposite side of the road is a cottage which was the home of an unfortunate child who perished from an adder sting between the wars.

"Slacken Bearing Rein", reads the notice beyond the Glaven bridge, for Holt Hill is steep, and even now motor cars find it difficult in icy weather. So, over the heath to the last milestone, near Burton's Cottage (he was a famous gamekeeper). Beyond is Holt Lows, the 120-acre common, and the Race Course, which was broken up after the 1810 Enclosure, and has become a thicket of young trees.

At length we come to Holt Obelisk, at the entering in of the town, where once was a gallows. Now there is a stone pillar (from an old gateway to Melton Park). It has a pineapple on top, and bears the legend "Norwich 21 miles".

The Norwich-Holt road was once a Turnpike. Roads have never been right to their contemporaries ; the motorway comes in for criticism in the same manner as did the miry track from place to place, when roads were a parish responsibility. In fact, roads were once merely rights of way between villages ; after bad weather, when the track was founderous, passengers had the right to take their beasts into neighbouring fields, even if they were "under corn". In winter time many roads were impassable for wheeled traffic, and with the economic and social changes of the eighteenth century, something had to be done about them. Turnpike Acts were passed, establishing Trusts to keep stretches of road in better order, the Norwich to Thetford Turnpike being one of the first in the country (1707). The Turnpikes began to be effective in the mid century, but Norfolk, after a good start, seems to have lagged behind. In 1781 there were only 239 miles of turnpike, but there were also "some great leading roads, which have mile-stones, and in other respects not less commodious for travelling".

The Turnpike Trusts were often incompetent, sometimes corrupt, and they had little power to alter the course of a road. Pack horses could take the shortest route up a slippery bank which was impassable for wheels ; drovers preferred a soft surface for their horses to tread upon rather than the firmer foundations of Mr. Macadam. An apothecary of eastern England found himself sinking into the mire,

21

but was reassured by a lad in an adjacent field. Deeper and deeper he sank. "I thought", exclaimed the apothecary, "you said the road had a good bottom ! "

"So that have", replied the lad, "but you haint come to it yet".

When coaches were first used they went at walking pace, being drawn by animals of the cart-horse type, but by 1761 the Norwich to London coach completed the journey in a day, if day it could be called, which began before cock-crow and ended after dark. In April 1775, Parson Woodforde travelled by post-chaise from London to Norwich to view his future parish of Weston Longville. The journey took from early morning to 11 o'clock at night, costing Woodforde and his friend about £5.17. This was the Parson's first visit to Norwich, which he declared to be "The finest city in England by far . . . the City Walls are also very perfect . . . On the Hills above the City stand many Wind Mills, about a dozen to be seen from the Castle Mount." Travel by coach must have been uncomfortable to say the least of it. Outside, passengers were exposed to all weathers. Some passengers found the motion sickening. On a June evening at 9 o'clock, Woodforde and his niece and servant left the Angel Inn at Norwich. "We had four inside passengers, a man of Norwich by name Hix, a Grocer, one Single Lady, and a Comical Woman and a little Boy, her Son. The Child was sick most part of the night, as was also the Single Woman. We travelled all night, some rain . . . We got to London (thank God) safe and well, about 5 o'clock this evening, to the Angel Inn in the Strand, where we drank tea, supped and slept."

Woodforde thanked God, for a coach journey was not without dangers. The Norwich coach was once attacked by highwaymen, and in a fight several people were killed. In 1780, Woodforde noted "many people were robbed between Norwich and Mattishall by two highwaymen. They were both known and very near being taken. I was lucky I did not go to Norwich last week." Later, the highwaymen were captured, and condemned to death, but very nearly succeeded in escaping from Norwich Castle. Sir John Turner wrote from Warham to the Earl of Linford in 1764 of a journey back from London, "Found the roads so bad, and the waters so much out, that it cost me three days to get home, which I don't remember it ever did before, and to add to my misfortunes, I got a bad cold in the head, which put me much out of order." This was in September.

Accidents happened to coaches, as they do to motor coaches to-day. In 1821 the "Morning Star" overturned at Scole, through the fault of the coachman ; there were three

22

inside, and nine outside, one man died of injuries. The driver of the Brandon to Wells coach fell from his seat on a bitter February night, benumbed from cold. This happened at Toftrees, but the passangers were unaware of it, for the horses continued across Hempton Green, along the narrow Fakenham Street to the appointed halt at the Crown Inn. Then there was the reprehensible practise of racing coaches.

By 1846, with the coming of the railway from Norwich to London, coaching between the two cities ceased. Famous inns fell back upon local patronage and continued thus until the motoring age. But intermediate roads were still busy with many curious vehicles, and the turnpikes were proving inadequate for the volume of traffic. Toll-gates every five miles were a hindrance, their keepers unpopular, as they came out of their several-windowed houses to demand money from all save pedestrians. Thus, on the turnpike from St. Benedict's Gate, Norwich to Swaffham in 1834, a coach, landau, barouche, gig, hearse, etc. had to pay 3d. For any dog cart, low cart, or truck, or carriage, the charge was 1d. A herd of cows was let through for 10d a score, and anticipating a new devastating age, 5s was payable on every carriage of any description propelled by steam, gas, or machinery.

The days of the turnpike were numbered, and in 1835 an Act was passed authorising the setting up of Highway Boards. Another Highway Act went through in 1862. At the meeting of the Norwich and Swaffham Turnpike Trustees at the "King's Head" at Dereham in 1871, a letter was read from the Secretary of State saying that the Trust could be continued till November 1872, but no longer. The next year, the Clerk produced the conveyances of some toll houses and gardens to several purchasers, and the Trust agreed to compensate its surveyor with £156 being three years' notice. Eventually, after 1888, the new County Councils took over roads.

Old people still speak of the Turnpike ; this applies to the Norwich-Cromer road. Some of the plain arched milestones are also relics of the turnpike age An Act of 1767 made the Thetford-Norwich Turnpike responsible for the erection of milestones and direction posts. There are some pleasing milestones on the Norwich to New Buckenham road, engraved with the distances from Norwich to London. When the Norfolk County took over, it put up milestones for a time, bearing its name, but they are sometimes hollow, angular affairs, made of metal. Their erection has long been discontinued.

Everybody knows that, to a pedestrian, miles may vary in length, and we have also a standard mile, so to speak, between two well-known stones, which we inherit from childhood. But the motorist gobbles up milestones as unconsidered trifles. To those who meander, they are pleasing reminders of a quieter age, when the road was white, with two deep ruts. In damp weather the surface made a satisfactory crunch underfoot ; in dry, the dust lay thick on the stout hedges. The sides of the road were ill-defined, and sometimes there was a grassy path. The flint and sand were good for potting ; in the banks were cool primroses, and, perhaps, a yellowhammer's nest with eggs marked in brownish purple. The road twisted away, a pale line across the landscape, so different from the dark, smooth, rather sinister, track of to-day. Here and there were heaps of flints for filling up holes, and men patiently cracking them up with hammers. It was dangerous for the eyes, and sometimes they wore goggles protected by a wire mesh.

Section Two
PLACES

c

Wiveton Church from Swallow Green, Cley (from a sketch, about 1930)

BACONSTHORPE

YEARS ago, when people spoke of "good" and "bad" villages, Baconsthorpe came into the first category. It is a plain parish, with a single street, but there is a remarkable spot in the wide fields not far away.

Two centuries past, if Parson Hewitt can be believed, Baconsthorpe was a model community. There were about 200 inhabitants, roughly the same as to-day. The rector was determined not to let the reputation of his parish be forgotten, for he wrote in 1780 "the curious would be glad to know the number, manners, employments, and circumstances of the inhabitants in days of old, but such knowledge is not attainable now. Therefore, that posterity may not complain of us, a present state of the parish is here subjoined."

The farmers were "all very industrious frugal men, and remarkable for their skill in husbandry, there is not one drone in the hive. The generality of them make hay when the sun shines, and occasionally work in the fields in the time of harvest. Their wives also are very notable for industry, frugality, and good house-wifery". Rents "for the larger farms did not exceed £130 annually, and some do not exceed £20". Even then, it was the fashion to consider that the day of the small farmer was passing; Hewitt adds: "Were all the farms in the kingdom occupied in a like manner, and divided upon a similar scale, there would be very little need of houses of Industry, no need of societies—no want of premiums for encouragement of agriculture."

The Reverend Mr. Hewitt noted that "the greatest part of the land is arable, nevertheless an hundred milch cows are kept in the village . . . Here are some very respectable tradesmen and mechanics (two blacksmiths, one carpenter, one wheelwright, one cooper, one shoemaker, one tailor, hatter and hosier) who live in a very comfortable and respectable manner. The labouring husbandmen in general are sober and industrious. The Poor's Rates are very moderate here". With rather an air of gratification, the rector records "there is no public-house, no relic of a sign-post in the parish". The Reverend Mr. Hewitt lived near the church, a little apart from the Street, in "an humble cottage of thatch". Before his time the rectory had been burnt down twice, once through lightning, and again through the wash-house chimney catching fire. After that it continued ruinous till 1770, when it was repaired by Mr. Hewitt and the parishioners at considerable expense. The church was also partly destroyed by the steeple falling down in 1739. Again, Hewitt came to the rescue, and it was "thoroughly and beautifully repaired" chiefly out of his pocket, in 1779. But in 1863 "some miscreants broke into the church and, after burning the large Bible and prayer book and many valuable papers, etc., carried off the altar cloth, the cushions of the pulpit and reading desk, and various other things, and have unfortunately never been discovered". Was Baconsthorpe still "good" or did they come from without the parish ?

In Mr. Hewitt's time there were 31 occupied houses in Baconsthorpe. "All the inhabitants are members of the Church of England, except one respectable, but not rich, family who are Presbyterians, but a difference of religious opinion causes no other differences here."

Still, in Baconsthorpe, there is a blacksmith, whose forge is crowded with farm implements waiting for attention, and he shoes horses too. The "Hare and Hounds", at the top of the Street, is within the boundary of the next village— Hempstead—but it is nearer the houses of Baconsthorpe.

It is not to view the Street that visitors come to Baconsthorpe nowadays. About half a mile away at the end of the track across the fields, set in a park-like meadow, is all that is left of the Old Hall (sign-posts call it Baconsthorpe Castle). These latter days it has been set in order by the Office of Works ; before that it was an ivy-clad ruin within the watery moat, and perhaps more appealing. People came there to pick snowdrops, white and pleasant in the damp grass. Here were the remains of a garden within the moat. Scraggy apple trees cast up blossom, box edging showed in the tangled undergrowth, and on a wild hedge were blue butterflies.

Outside the moat is a house with a single turret, built from the original gate-house. Till 1920 it was occupied by a farmer and his family. Then, one night in early January, the occupants of the new hall were startled by a loud rumble, and found that the west wing of the building had collapsed. It was thought that the great August flood of 1912 had undermined the foundations and caused the disaster.

If no unpleasant people dwelt in Baconsthorpe in Parson Hewitt's time there had been one before him. A Paston called John Heydon "a false shrew". He is said to have incited a riot of 1,000 to break in and despoil the Paston manor house at Gresham. He was accused of threatening his own wife, brought to bed of a child, "to cut off her nose, and make her know what she was, and kill the child". John

Heydon was a lawyer and politician, a typical product of the chaotic England of the Wars of the Roses ; he was likened to Pontious Pilate. His father had bought land at Baconsthorpe, and John had begun to build the defensive house there before his death in 1480.

John's son, Henry, was a considerable improvement upon his father, and was approved of by the Pastons. He finished erecting the Baconsthorpe house. He had another at West Wickham in Kent. The church there contains a window showing him rising at the Last Judgement, and the words "Remember not our sins nor the sins of our fathers."

He built the magnificent church at Salthouse, and made a causeway between Thursford and Walsingham. His son, Sir John, was knighted at the coronation of Henry VIII. At first he was a spendthrift, "but at length he became a great husband". Two generations later, we find Sir Christopher Heydon called "the great Housekeeper of Norfolk". He was a notable flockmaster, and is said to have entertained thirty of his master-shepherds to Christmas dinner at Baconsthorpe. But his son, William, got involved with London speculators, and had to sell some of his estates.

At the time of the Civil War, a Sir John Heydon was a staunch supporter of King Charles I, whose Lieutenant-General of Ordnance he was. His estates were afterwards sequestrated by the Cromwellians, but he was allowed to buy them back. To make good some of his losses, he pulled down most of the Baconsthorpe house, and the stone was sold to the Felbrigg estate. The last Heydon died in 1689. He had sold the Old Hall, or what remained of it, to a London woollen draper. The latter went bankrupt, and the estate passed to a doctor with the astonishing name of Zurishaddai Lang, who was probably the first to occupy the building which had been made out of the gate-house. But the Heydons had lasted over 200 years at Baconsthorpe, in the male line, a considerable time for an English family in affluence.

CLEY-NEXT-THE-SEA

IT IS one of the surprising sights of Norfolk—the three churches seen all at once, a mile apart, by the northern shore. There is Blakeney behind the trees, looking like some great monster with its tail up, Wiveton, a cannon barrel before it, and Cley huddled massively on the slope, with the tower peeping over the nave. Any county would be proud of the trio. Comparisons may be odious, but Cley church seems to have the greatest attraction. Looking over the quiet Glaven valley, it is a relic of a different ancient scene which is partly restored "once in a lifetime", when the sea breaks in, roads and bridges disappear ; centuries melt away, and the church stands again above the water. Wiveton, on the opposite side of the valley, has similarly gone back in time. But in the modern transformation there are no ships, no people at the busy quays, only worried folks whose homes are very wet and maybe ruined by the flood. Those who come to aid them from away are uncertain whether to call the village Cly or Clay ; even locally some say one and some the other, but Domesday Book wrote Claia.

For long Cley has been spoken of as being in a decline. A visitor in 1828 said "The harbour is very bad, there not being sufficient water." Somebody else noted in 1780, "Cley does not appear ever to have been of any eminence. The channel to the sea is very narrow and navigable only by very small ships such as sloops, etc."

Of course he was wrong ; in the 14th and 15th centuries Cley was a busy port, exporting wool to the Low Countries, and trading elsewhere. Its prosperity lessened when weaving increased at home, but it was still an important place. Cardinal Wolsey ordered a shipment of supplies for the army at Calais from here, and "dried cod from Wm. Momfort of Cley." In Queen Elizabeth's reign, Cley had 69 mariners and 13 ships, 2 of them over 100 tons (Wiveton had 4) whilst Lynn had but 2 of the same size. There was much coastal trade, and local mariners faced the rough seas of Iceland, probably after whale.

A severe blow struck the port of Cley in the time of Charles I. Sir Phillip Calthorpe built a bank across the valley (near the present Cley-Blakeney road) stopping access of ships to the higher Cley and Wiveton quays. "Whereas in 1637, 30 entries of ships are recorded in the customs house, only 14 made entry in 1638 . . . The country for want of coals, etc. were enforced to give far greater prices than formerly." A petition from the inhabitants was successful— the offending bank was demolished, but silting had increased. Thereafter matters got worse, till the old inner waterway was sealed off finally under an Enclosure Act of 1823. After that, the tidal marshes gradually turned into fresh grazing land.

The twisting village street with its old houses is very pleasing to-day. Here is the old Customs House, which once served the ports of both Blakeney and Cley. The present Cley creek was made after the 1914-18 war, replacing a former one which had become blocked. This, in its turn, no longer gives access to the main Blakeney channel and the open sea, owing to the encroaching shingle bank.

* * * * *

Cley had its marauders. In 1619, it was the only port on the coast which made a contribution for the suppression of pirates. Then later, in 1825, the Commissioners of Customs were offering a £100 reward for the capture of other molesters. "A large party of men unknown were assembled within the port of Cley for the purpose of landing a quantity of Foreign Spirits from a Boat which was close to the beach. That George Monkman and John Nicholls, Boatmen in the Preventive Service, were patrolling the Coast, and detained in the said Boat, the two men they were endeavouring to secure, when the aforesaid party beat them severely with bludgeons, leaving Nicholls almost lifeless on the Sand, and keeping Monkman a Prisoner, threatening they would kill him, till daybreak appearing, the said party disappeared."

Back to the church by Newgate Green, away from the centre of the village ; once it was more central, but houses were destroyed by a 17th-century fire. Upon its green stance, above all possible floods, past or present, is humped the great church ; in its different styles, generations are symbolised in stone. The tower is older than the rest of the building ; it served a former church. and has stood there 600 years. As Cley increased in prosperity, a grander church was designed, with arcades rising to clerestories ornamented with cinquefoil and lancet windows. Aisles were built, and a north and south transept. But there was no roof when a disaster occurred which few can have anticipated—the Black Death. Work was stopped for a hundred years. Then the building was finished, and the church looked much as it does to-day, but not quite, for there had been transepts. Now, only the roofless walls of one remains. As Cley diminished as a port, the parishioners were "hard put" to maintain the great fabric.

Passing to-day through the beautiful south porch, decorated with armorial bearings, and with empty niches from which Cromwell's men dragged out the saints, one is suddenly enveloped in the great church. Somebody said it put him in mind of a "lovely lady in a shabby dress". For though there was a Victorian restoration of the roof, the general impression is of great age. The floor is mottled with original stone, square red bricks, and there are tombstones black and shiny in damp weather . . . In the midst of the west end is a stout seven-sacrament font. The great height of the nave rising to the clerestory, towers above the beholder, who is caught up in the silences of time. Restoration is imperative, to the tune of £20,000, if the great church is to remain standing, and it is not only a Norfolk but a national memorial.

DOINGS AT DISS

THE market town of Diss is just over a mile from the railway station, which was built in 1847. It is a long walk on a hot day, and there is a cold windy platform on which to wait for one's train in winter. On the opposite side of the road is the "Jolly Porters". At one time this public house was the resort of drovers waiting for the cattle train from Norwich, after the Saturday market, and quarrels often broke out between them, resulting in violent scenes. In the early days, cattle had to be driven through the "park fields" in order to cross the River Waveney into Suffolk by a shorter route, and the road through was for pedestrians only. There were two sets of 7-ft. gates at about 200 yards distant from each other. These were kept locked, and one had to obtain permission (and the keys) from the Lord of the Manor. He lived in a Georgian house in Mount Street, which is still standing and occupied by one of his descendants (1970).

Driving cattle, sheep, and pigs, through this private road was an exciting business on a dark night. On one side the road was fenced by iron railings, and the other comprised a thorn fence. Sheep especially were a lot of trouble. There were lush meadows on this latter side, intersected by becks and dykes running into the river ; one sheep would notice a small hole in the fence, and would squeeze through, closely followed by all the others. Rounding them up would often take the best part of an hour, by which time the drovers had very wet feet and legs. In earlier days, cattle and sheep were all driven straight through Mere Street, the main shopping district, to the great discomfort of lady-shoppers, who had to gather up their long skirts and make a dash for the nearest shop, there to remain till the cattle had passed by.

Diss has all the elements of most old market towns ; there are colour-washed houses and some larger ones in white, all grouped on a hill on which most of the town stands ; together with all this, the twin towers of the Baptist Church and the gardens and orchards sloping down gradually to the Mere of about 5½ acres, form a scene of great beauty.

About 1880, there were as many as 24 inns and hotels in Diss, and also 12 different places of worship. One could say that the town was well served with pubs and pulpits !

33

One of the older and more picturesque streets
in this ancient Market Town

(June 1971)   St. Nicholas Street, Diss.   *(Photo : K. W. Webster)*

LOOKING down St. Nicholas Street one is amazed at how it
has retained its ancient character for so many years whilst
modernization and rebuilding are taking place in many
other parts of the town.

The buildings, are, for the most part just as they were
over 80 years ago, of course, the names over the shop fronts
have changed, except when the trading names have been
retained for business reasons, or where old family businesses
are still being carried on by the sons or grand-sons of the
original owners.

The Greyhound Inn is famous for its carved staircase
and Jacobean plaster work.

The shop on the corner, facing the viewer, was, in 1890
occupied by William Fry Barnes, a watchmaker and
jeweller.

St. Nicholas Street is a continuation of Crown Street
and in these two streets almost every trade and craft was
represented.

The "Greyhound" and "Saracen's Head" are very old buildings, and well worth a visit. Diss church stands near the Market Place, and was founded by Sir Robert Fitzwilliam in the reign of King John. It is said the King coveted Sir Robert's daughter, and because he could not get her, he had her poisoned.

John Skelton was rector of Diss in the early part of the 16th century. He had been tutor to Henry VIII and became Poet Laureate. His writings were full of satire, and he made many enemies. One of these, named Lilly, wrote—

> *"Whilst Skelton thou to get esteem,*
> *A learned poet fain would seem ;*
> *Skelton, thou art, let all men know it,*
> *Neither learned nor a poet."*

At the time of the great plague, Diss suffered grievously, fifty-six people dying in one year, and, according to the custom, church bells were rung to drive away the evil spirits. . . "It is said that evyl speryts havinge ben in ye regyon of ye ayre do doubte moche when they heare ye bells rongen that wycked speryts may be constrayned and cease from their troublings of all goode soulys for certyn."

Originally, the church had six bells and a "sanctus" bell, which occupied the turret of the church between the chancel and the nave. It was inscribed : *Sancte Gabriel Dra pro nobis,* and when the workhouse was built (which in later years was converted into almhouses) the "Sanctus" bell was taken from the church to the workhouse and used for calling the inmates to their meals.

*　*　*　*　*

At a very early period, Diss had two guilds, namely : "St. Nicholas" and "Corpus Christi". There was also a Weavers' Guild, which held its meetings in a large room at the "Saracen's Head" hotel. All Guild members were known as "Gildens" and had to pay a certain sum yearly, in order that they could carry out the purposes of the guild to which they belonged.

The merchant guilds were licensed by the King and each was governed by its own laws. There are records and deeds at the time of Richard II, giving some details of the "Jolly Doings" when the brethren met to "eat, drink and be merry" Doubtless they were disciples of those who sang :

> *"Let schoolmasters puzzle their brains*
> *With grammar, nonsense and learning ;*
> *Good liquor I stoutly maintain*
> *Gives genius a better discerning."*

35

The Guildhall, Diss, about 1843

Diss Guildhall stood (until 1843) at the south-east corner of the churchyard, and this, together with the large timbered houses in the vicinity, denoted that the town benefited from the wool and cloth trade in the late middle ages. The Shambles in the Market Place was at one time composed of two butchers' shops, one of which is now a local museum. "The Mustard Pot" was a tall building standing by itself in the Market Place, but, alas, it is no longer there !

Friday is market day in Diss, and there is a large attendance of farmers and their wives. The corn market is held in the "Greek Revival" Corn Hall and cattle are sold in the "Saracen's Head" yard and at Apthorp's sale ground ; until recently, an annual lamb sale was held, attended by buyers from all over the country. Whilst the farmers are on business, their wives are out in the town doing their shopping. The shopping centre is much more modern than the old, handsome part of Diss. There have been latter-day improvements. The mouth of the Mere and the Park have received a "new look". Now visitors can sit at the Mere's mouth and feed the swans and other birds.

Market Hill was once called Pump Hill because, seventy years ago, there was a pump there, with an apparatus for filling the water-cart which, before the days of tarmac, sprayed the dusty streets in dry weather. The cart was nearly always followed by a crowd of small boys who liked wetting their legs on a warm summer's day.

The mere at Diss was nearly always frozen over during the winter months and, in 1895, there were 12 weeks of frost. A grand carnival was held in which there were skating competitions in fancy dress, with parades of decorated tradecarts and horses ; also, there were decorated and illuminated bicycles from "penny-farthings" to "bone-shakers", and the very latest "balloon-tyred" models. The bills were printed by Messrs. Lusher Brothers. Nothing of the same kind ever took place on the mere after that time, as the ice has never been thick enough to withstand so much weight. Many skating carnivals have been held, but very minor affairs compared with the Carnival of 1895—a year which was later to have some of the most severe gales in living memory. Stacks had to be held down by tarpaulins and ropes tied to tree trunks. This was in March ; many of the stacks were still unthreshed, and their loss would have been a calamity, as insurance was then almost unknown for farm animals, corn or other stock-in-trade of the farmer.

*   *   *   *   *

It was customary in Diss to hold a Gala and Sports on August Bank Holiday ; flags and streamers would fly on the church steeple and the bells would ring preceding the event. On one occasion (about 1901), an extra special sports had been arranged—steam horses, and all side-shows ; sports, including running, jumping, and cycle races, climbing the greasy pole, catching the pig (greased all over), obstacle races, etc. ; and refreshments were on sale in large marquees. Then, at the end of the sports, the star turn of the day, a balloon ascent by the "Professor" who was to descend by parachute. The balloon was filled and all ready to go up, when the "Professor" said he would not ascend unless the Committee gave him another £5. The Committee dared not disappoint the 5,000 or more spectators who had come from all over Norfolk, so they paid up. When the body of men who were holding down the balloon got the signal from the "Professor" to let go, the balloon went straight up into the air until it looked about the size of a football. Everybody cheered loudly, and then the spectators watched as a white object appeared and presently assumed the shape of a parachute, and was slowly descending. The envelope of the balloon, from which the gas was now issuing, descended also, assuming all kinds of shapes as it became more and more limp, until finally it dropped on some soft marshland. The parachute, however, was not so lucky, and it dropped into a large tree in a plantation nearby, from which the "Professor" had to be rescued. The day closed with a cinematograph display, showing various comic films.

37

At one time, numerous German bands in olive green uniform would tour the country, and play to people even in remote villages, They were very popular until Germany became somewhat bellicose, and started a battleship race with Britain. Then someone spread it around that these bands might be just a cover for spying activities. This attitude caught on, and the next time they appeared in Diss they were hustled out of the town by some ex-army men, and forced to get on the next train. This was the beginning of the end of German bands.

*   *   *   *   *

The "Fair Green" must have been used for fairs and other similar gatherings for hundreds of years. An article appearing in the *Waveney Valley Weekly News* of 1872 states that there were two fairs at Diss each year, one called the "Sessions", held in the Market Place in September, "Cocking" taking place at the Cock Inn near Fair Green, and "Bull Baitings" in the Market Place, where there was a bull-ring. The other was held in November. Diss is said to have been somewhat dull except at "Cockings" and "Baitings" and Fairs.

The interest taken in Diss Fairs about 150 years ago may be seen from the diary of a gentleman who lived at Ipswich at the time.

Footbridge and Ford over the River Waveney at the end of Cock Street, near Fair Green, in the early 1800's

"Saturday November 6, 1817. Arrived at Scole Inn by coach this afternoon. The place all alive on account of Diss Fair. The Norwich coach arrived bringing with it several 'coves' I met last year.

"We drank success to the fair, just then the landlord came in, and we asked him what frolics there were for next week's fair . . . 'They tell me the cocking begins on Sunday night'. But one of our number interrupted and said, 'I thought the constables threatened to put down Sunday cocking'. I don't think the constables 'll interfere, but some o' they Methodys might, Tom Lee, their preacher for instance.' 'Not if they value their limbs' said another, 'but he's a stiff little fello' and heeds not a thump or two' . . .

"Sunday. To-day had a walk over to Diss with two characters from Norwich . . . Preparations were in hand on Fair Green by the show men and others, there being a fine stock of merry-go-rounds, swing boats, sideshows, and booths, for provisions and beer. There was no 'cocking' on account of there being but a few entries.

"Monday. This morn I went to Diss at an early hour. The day had fully broken and there was promise of fair weather. The green was rapidly filling with people in holiday gear. There appeared to be something like a 1,000 walking round . . . A clown in grotesque attire was haranguing the crowd with plenteous wit ; dancing girls with tambourines and showmen standing outside the sideshows calling, 'Walk up, walk up'. One such show had a pair of giant bloomers flying at the top of a tall pole, and showmen were shouting and beating a drum. 'Walk up, walk up, come and see your Aunt Susan's thighs, the biggest thighs on the fair.' All this being greeted by loud laughter and course jokes by the peasantry.

"It was still morning and presently there was a rush towards the cockpit, where two famous birds were to fight it out. Ben Moseley came in carrying his bird 'Red Cap'. Never did I see such splendid plumage. He was of great size, and had his comb clipped and claws steeled ready for battle. The owners handled their birds as tenderly as if they had been small children.

"Inside the place was crowded to suffocation, there being no windows, it was lighted by torches, which shone on people's faces with a sickly glare . . . it became Red Cap's turn to battle with the Champion, a mighty fine bird from Kenninghall. This was the fight of the day, and many guineas depended on it. At first Red Cap was shy, and got punished badly by the Champion, but presently Red Cap struck his steel into the Champion, and there was immediately a cry of 'first blood'. Then the struggle became

39

intense . . . for about a quarter of an hour. At last the Champion made a desperate plunge which laid Red Cap panting on the floor. Poor bird, his feathers were clotted with blood, an eye was almost out of its socket, he was but a wreck of his former glory. I turned to go, thoroughly sickened by the savagery of this contest. The settling of bets caused great confusion and uproar. On the green I found some engaged in bear baiting and drawing the badger. I paused for a few minutes to gaze upon a surly old bear on a chain, dancing to a tune played by his keeper on a concertina . . . Then to the bear-baiting, where a savage-looking bear was setting its eyes on a bull-pup . . ." (The details of this contest are too nasty to repeat.)

"For some purpose unknown to me, the bull-baiting this year took place on Fair Green . . . and was due to start just after midday, so I took me into a booth where sausages on a round of toast were in great demand at sixpence. The place was full of rough fellows, dealers and others, carrying whip stalks, ready for defending themselves if the occasion arose. It was soon shown that a man must keep a tight hold on his sausages and toast once he had them in his grasp . . . Thinking discretion the better part of valour, I made my way out of the tent, foregoing the merits or demerits of this homely meal. Making my way to the Bull Ring, I saw the noble animal tethered to a stake, behind a stockade of sharp-topped poles . . . Glancing shyly at first, the dog seemed almost fearful of attacking, but goaded on by its owner it rushed toward its enormous foe . . ." (The details of that encounter are as horrible as may be imagined), but at the end of it, the now infuriated and badly bleeding bull . . . making one desperate plunge, broke the tether, and dashed wildly among the people . . . The bravest men turned pale, and the terror of the women and children knew no bounds. The crowd scattered in all directions . . . in a moment the 'Green' was a scene of utter confusion—apple stalls were overturned upon their owners—mountebanks threw down their instruments and fled for their lives ; then, to crown all, a fearful thunder storm which had been threatening for some time, burst o'er the scene. The rain fell in torrents, with vivid lightning, and the thunder crashed like falling mountain crags, giving the scene a most terrible aspect. I shall never forget the scene, it has been one of the most eventful of my life, and I should not care to see another like it."

Here the narrative ends, and one cannot but be thankful that such days of cruelty in sports and pastimes have passed away.

DOTSELL (Briston)

SEEN from the *black* main road, Dotsell (that is not the real name) is hardly an attractive village, with its line of slate-roofed council houses, which were tarred over in the war, sombre objects indeed. On the side road there is a hotch-potch of Victorian buildings, with here and there a more graceful house put up before that grim period. The church lacks a steeple, for it was pulled down three centuries ago, and in its place is a niche containing a bell ; on the Green, the coloured top of a merry-go-round is a cheering sight. Dotsell is a big parish of 2955 acres, and 1200 inhabitants, who do not all live in the Street, but in the deep out-of-the-way fringe.

Mist had rolled in from the sea, dimming the verdant leaves and chilling everybody in the Street, but as the intruder penetrated a very narrow side road down to the bridge over the *Blackwater,* the sun came out and there was sweetness abroad. A very green bank was mottled with primroses, and the carressing sound of a turtle dove came from the trees. The road sloped out of the dip, and off it was a field-path leading to a bridge which spanned a disused railway track. The cutting had a skin of turf and a riot of brambles and flowering gorse ; beyond the bridge was a precipitous pit full of trees, and beside it a funnel of lush grass falling very steeply through the wood.

The intruder in the motor car was worried—there was no room to turn ; it was a bit perilous to back. In the end, the driver edged the car down the steep grass slope. The path turned at the bottom, and there was a great meadow ; beyond a beck, the land curved up to a house. A herd of black-and-white bullocks straggled towards the closed gate. The intruder left the car, climbed into the meadow, and walked towards the house, followed discreetly by the bullocks.

On the brow of the hill was a wire. The housewife came out of the doorway. "Don't touch it," she called, "that's electric." Within the wire was a group of geese with their necks up, and a pen of goslings. "You didn't come along that there ol' right o' way ? ", asked the housewife incredu-lously. She went back with the intruder across the meadow which stretched endlessly on either side into soft distance of swamp and trees ; a cuckoo called. "I've been in hospital

41

Long Tom Tipple, shot dead by a neighbour

having my teeth out," said the housewife, but the world of
wards and urban places seemed very far away. "Fifteen year
I've lived here. That's quiet but I like it." The bullocks
were hushed off, and native and intruder drove back towards
the house. "Mind you keep off them tracks do you'll get
stuck fast," she warned.

There was another way out of Arcadia, a long, long track,
pale from drought, but before it ended a loke opened off to
the right, tempting the intruder to find another Arcadia.
This turned out to be a small plain house under the lee of
the land, and beyond it an enclosure of rough herbage to the
valley bottom. The yard was littered with various tools of
husbandry, some stout, various-coloured hens and a bantam
cock. "What do you call this place ? " asked the intruder.
The farmer smiled, "I dussent tell you," he said. He led
the way into a small old barn. Some young pigs occupied
one side, and a sow reclined in her pen on the other. The
man patted her affectionately. "She's going to have her first
litter next week."

The headwaters of the Bure slipped by 30 yards below the
house, and a narrow plank spanned the stream to the yielding
thicket on the other side. "My boys put that there," he said.
"They've a long way to go to school, two mile on the bikes
to Dotsell Green, and then ten in the bus. Anyhow, my
mortgage is paid, and this is a good sheltered place to live in.
Never noticed the wind when the sea came through in '53.
Funny thing, my ol' dawg—he's tied up—haint barked at
you."

So back from Arcadia came the intruder, back into the
cold fret, which was still obscuring the village street.

*   *   *   *   *

In the last century Dotsell was what was known as an
"open" parish, without a big landlord, and charitable doles.
Those who were against the Establishment, and got the sack,
the poorest of the poor, the wilder of the wild, and some of
the most virile folk, drifted into Dotsell. Some lived in
shacks on the edge of commons (there were big commons
before enclosure) getting a few days' employment now and
then. Small landlords put up inferior houses, and let them
to families no big estate would accept. Between 1831-41
principal parishioners sent 150 paupers to Canada.

But there were advantages in living in an "open" village.
Men could speak their minds without fear of squire or parson,
and organise their own chapels—there were four different
denominations in Dotsell. Even in the present century,
unusual characters were to be found in the village, such as
the man who cured warts by cutting notches in a stick, and

who was consulted by many, and the editor of a famous London newspaper who drove down from Town in his horse-drawn carriage, to the white house in the paddock.

Dotsell had a swine market every Tuesday, a large cattle fair on May 26th and a "wake" (or frolic) the day after Michaelmas, which was a hiring fair for yearly servants. Also, Dotsell had, and still has, a spring with medicinal properties, and a doctor used to advise patients to fill bottles with the water, and drink it to relieve their ailments. Then there was Long Tom Tipple, who was a sort of pedlar, and a dealer in rags and scrap metal. One day, in old age, he was moved to climb upon his neighbour's roof and start pulling off the tiles. Whereupon the neighbour, also an aged man, came out with a gun and shot him dead. So that was the end of Tom Tipple, but the neighbour was not hanged but sent to the Asylum. Altogether, Dotsell is a place of character.

EDGEFIELD AND THE PARSONS

EDGEFIELD is not particularly remote, and a "B" road runs by the Green. Its name describes it, though it is derived from a "park or pasture". But Edgefield is a distinctive parish, and has had two remarkable parsons. Few strangers who drive past the Green know of the existence of Ramsgate Street, pressed into its shallow valley, and parellel to the main Norwich-Saxthorpe road. From the upper end of the Street the church pops up over the meadow, and it has not been there so very long ; the Rev. W. H. Marcon moved it to this central site of the scattered parish in 1883-85. Only the octagonal tower of the old church remains on the distant slope of the Glaven valley. It rears up from amongst the nettles which hide the tombstones, and a blue pigeon perches in a lancet window. Above, in the woods, is an artificial mound made for a warning beacon at the time of the Armada.

The original church had become dilapidated ; lead from the roof had been stripped off in 1827 to pay for repairs to the rest of the fabric. For well or ill, Parson Marcon was determined to move it, though some of his parishioners did not like the idea. The enterprise cost nearly £2000, much of which was raised by Marcon's personal effort, but a parishioner took care he should not feel too pleased with himself. "That's your hobby, you like doing of it, same as I do my hobby—buying bullocks."

Hubert Marcon was born in Edgefield Rectory in 1850, and succeeded his father as Rector by popular request in 1876. He was tall and lean, a great cyclist, who once rode to Land's End and back. Towards the end of his long life people would think that he was dozing as he went by. Hubert Marcon observed and recorded all his life. He had seen the reapers moving in echelon across the harvest field, the first man being called the lord. After harvest, young men decorated their caps with ribbons, and went round the village "A-hallerin' largess." This was a very old custom certainly practised two centuries before.

Many a labouring man and his brood lived in a hovel with a 5½ ft. doorway, windows not worth the name, and a steep ladder in a recess near the fireplace, leading to a couple of rooms above. Things changed in Marcon's time. He saw

The Rev. Hubert Marcon, of Edgefield

fifty such dwellings demolished, and in 1914 a row of Council houses was put up, each with half an acre of garden. The Parson fought hard for half an acre, not a quarter, for he knew how a poor family depended upon vegetables to eke out its meagre diet. The Parson was a friend of everybody in the parish, no matter of what denomination ; he was acquainted with every staircase and dog, but he drew the line at cats !

In his early days, Edgefield was a wild, lawless, place, and many people were born, lived, and died there without ever going beyond the bounds. Now it welcomes strangers, but even as late as 1910 a family which moved in from the village of Hunworth had a cold reception. Moreover, folk from the Green did not keep company with those from the Street.

The Edgefield motto was "Never you know nathin', nobody can't git over that." Poachers were out on dark nights. Also Marcon was told, "I ha' known the time when I used to have to go for ol' W.W. down to Blakeney quay, to get a cargo o' liquor. Anybody with a hoss and cart used to go. All our hosses and carts would rattle down on the Quay, where the tubs stood. There'd be hundreds on 'em. An' they'd be all on the carts and gone in a quarter of an hour. Then as soon as ever we were out of the town you could hear the guns of the Preventive men a blazin' away arter us. Du they never hit us, not they ! Cos why ? That was all a planned thing, that wuz ; they knew where to find a keg for their selves. We'd got 2s. 6d. a night. Sometimes we'd have to go 10 nights afore the ship cam' in, and then we'd get 5s. apiece. Why ! in this house where we're now settin', I ha' seen the chamber right cram full o' casks . . . And we allust left a keg inside the Parson's gate here."

Parson Marcon was the first chairman of the new Parish Council of Edgefield, he was Rural Dean, and an honorary canon ; but his parishioners valued most his kindness to one and all. When death caught up with him, he died in the same room in which he had been born 86 years before, and he had been rector for 60.

That reverend gentleman, Bransby Francis, is beyond the links of living memory, but he was Rector of Edgefield from 1764 to 1829, beating Hubert Marcon's reign by five years, and he died at the age of ninety. It is known that he used the tithe barn as a school for children, and taught there with his daughter. Also, he had quite an adequate dinner with Parson Woodforde and others at Norwich in April 1784 There was "a Dish of Fish, Rump of Beef boiled, Veal Cutlets with forced Balls, a Turkey roasted and some Lemon Creams." His wife, astonishingly enough, had "great

47

proficiency in the Hebrew language", and was the author, amongst other works, of *A Poetical Translation of the Song of Solomon,* and a *Collection of Miscellaneous Poems.* She died in 1800.

Edgefield to-day has a population of around 400, much the same as at the beginning of the century, when there were other notable inhabitants besides the Parson—William Hagen, who looked rather like John Bull, and lived in a very ancient farmhouse with a secret room. At the Walnut Tree Farm was Tom Potter, who wore a small white beard and side whiskers. He was one of the first to grow bearded wheat in Norfolk, lived to 96, and went out shooting the year before. For some strange reason the visiting donkey would stand by the walnut tree without being tied up.

Inside a wing of the house was a stone-floored kitchen, and a great open fireplace, with a door beside it, opening on to the rotting staircase, which led to a windowless chamber. The living-room had drugget on the floor, and mounted cow's horns above a doorway. It was a mystery why the bread and butter at Tom's tasted so much nicer than that at home! The house still stands, with its sweeping roof, and sweet complacency of old England, but the walnut tree has been cut down, and now they call it Potter's Farm.

Then there was Mrs. Temple, a farmer's widow, who lived well and so did her cats, for she made them a custard with eight eggs. And still there is Lucy in her railway carriage. Her garden, between the smooth hedges, has a surprising assortment of fruit, vegetables, flowers and beehives, and here is the strange little hen that lays eggs the size of pigeon's! She says "I'd rather have been born when I wuz. Times were hard them days, but there was a sense of achievement they hain't got now."

GROUP OF PARISHES

"Gimingham, Trimingham, Knapton, Trunch,
Northrepps, Southrepps, lie all in a bunch."

THUS goes the old rhyme, and these east Norfolk villages are
bunched together in more than one sense. The scenery of
this neighbourhood is distinctive, but it is difficult to say why.
Even in calm weather there are reminders of the prevailing
wind in the solitary, stunted trees, with their grotesque
trailing tops. The wide view of fields is cut off abruptly at
the cliff edge.

Standing back from the road at Gimingham is a very old
house. Once it stood there neglected in age, gaunt and
forlorn, with mouldering thatch. Now, the roof is mended,
and there is a lawn before the door ; in the garden are
cloves and bergamot. It was probably a Tudor-built house,
new when the Soke of Gimingham was already ancient. The
Soke was a jurisdictional area, including the villages of the
rhyme and Mundesley and Sidestrand as well. In the reign
of Edward I, John, Earl of Warren and Surrey, was lord of
the Soke of Gimingham, holding it of the King by the
peculiar tenure of a mushroom or fungus. He claimed,
amongst other privileges, a gallows, wreck of the sea, and
assize of bread and beer, which meant that everybody within
the Soke had to buy these commodities within its boundaries,
and have their corn ground at the mill. Afterwards the
Soke passed to the House of Lancaster, and formed part of
the Duchy of Lancaster for centuries.

At Gimingham there was once a manor house with "a very
large hall, supported by several pillars, and the custom and
rule was that no tenant or soc-man, etc. should go beyond
that pillar which was appointed for their station and degree".
Of Clement, one of the early and humble Paston family, it
was said "that he had at Paston (a neighbouring parish) a five
scores or six scores acres of land, and much thereof bond land
to Gymingham Hall." Clement Paston had the "poor little"
mill at Gimingham.

Apart from the village, stands the old workhouse, which
is now divided into dwellings. A sombre red building, it
tones into the landscape, and was built in 1805 to accommodate upwards of 250 persons, "a House of Industry" to serve

49

the six villages of the rhyme, and Mundesley, Sidestrand, and Overstrand as well.

Above Gimingham, with its check-board of fields, is Trimingham, on the highest cliff in Norfolk. "From the beacon, or rather the place where the beacon once stood, you have a most extensive prospect of both sea and country, both Yarmouth and Norwich spires being distinctly seen", wrote somebody in the 18th century. "The overflowing of the sea makes every year a powerful impression upon the scene." However it was reckoned to be a subterraneous volume of water which caused the downfall of two farmhouses. One stood for several weeks after the first; then a crack was discovered to seaward. A haystack stood upon the separated part, which the owner determined to remove; scarcely had the wheels of his waggon, carrying the last load, cleared the crack, when the whole piece gave way.

In the will of one named Cooke of Horstead, 1478, is "Item, I wyll have a man go a pilgrimage to St. John hys hede of Trymmyngham." But this must not be taken to have been a genuine relic of the saint. There was probably an alabaster head set up in the church as an object of devotion.

Knapton and Trunch, the southernmost villages of the Soke, have such splendid churches that their names are familiar to people outside the county. The angels of the double hammerbeam roof at Knapton seem about to bear the building aloft, but among the medieval craftsmanship of Trunch, the fancy lingers for a moment at a memorial of more recent origin. "To the memory of George Ward . . . A Youth of most amiable manners and promising hopes, who died of a fever off Brest on board H.M.S. Dragon on which he served from Aug. 8th 1798 to the day of his death on the 4th March 1800 in the 17th year of his age."

The Repps, North and South, are said to have given their names to the cloth, for Flemish weavers settled here. A visitor to Northrepps at the beginning of the last century wrote, "On an emminence called Toll's Hill is a very fine echo . . . by descending into the vallies, the hills are brought to fold over each other, and the land between them and the sea, being interspersed with cottages and a few trees (the latter scarce near the sea) render the situation very picturesque." Below Toll's Hill, at the Hermitage, the Cottage Ladies, Sarah Buxton and Anna Gurney, sat in their parlour, which was decorated with marine plants and shells. Sarah was the sister of Sir Fowell Buxton, the philanthropist who was associated with Elizabeth Fry in prison reform, and with Wilberforce in the abolition of slavery. Fowell often appealed to the Cottage Ladies for help and advice. Like them, he was renowned locally for his kindness. "When asked by a poor neighbour to buy a joint of pork he would buy two, one for himself and one for the seller. It is a cruel thing, he would say, for the poor labourer to part with all his pig." Sarah Buxton died in 1839, but Anna, who had been a cripple most of her life, survived for nearly 18 years. She was the friend of fishermen and sailors, experimented with life-saving apparatus, and cared for shipwrecked crews.

Fowell Buxton died in 1845, but his widow lived on at Northrepps Hall, which was indeed a pleasant place, with brilliant foreign birds living and nesting in the woods. His daughter wrote in July 1855, "This place is in great beauty. Honeysuckles are still in flower, and the white Banksia rises over the gables. The annuals overflow the beds, and are splendid in the bright sunshine. The scarlet lowery flew down to greet us. The young cockatoos are delighted to follow us about the garden. (July 12th) The hay is being made, and the school children are coming to play in it, an express was sent to Cromer for plenty of strawberries and milk for their supper. This has been spread on the lawn". On July 30th, the children were again to tea on the lawn. "Two new parrots have been added to our flock today. We have put them in cages out of doors. I have let the parroquets come out and join the others on the trees, which they have done with great satisfaction. (Aug. 13th.) The little girls are crowding round the cistern of water, while Francis is eagerly pumping, and a cockatoo is sitting on the edge of the tub . . ."

Lady Buxton, the sister of Elizabeth Fry, did not die till 1872 in her 90th year. She was a remarkable and religious person ; when 81 she wrote to her brother, "Surely goodness and mercy have followed me since I was born at Bramerton in 1783 ! What a course I have run, and what blessings I have enjoyed ; and yet how severe my trials and innumerable my losses ! Today I go on picnic with children but far more grandchildren ; with these I am encompassed, but do not mind the numbers for myself. I rather feel for the servants, often more than sixty to feed in the day."

HUNSTANTON

THE fascination of Hunstanton is the distant shore, far away enough to be slightly fabulous. Sometimes it is not there, for the sea looks like a blob of ink on blotting paper, fading into oblivion. Or the water may be silver-bright in the evening sun, with only a faint rim upon the horizon. Occasionally, Lincolnshire reveals its secrets, plain, dark woods behind, and Boston Stump.

In the earlier days of New Hunstanton, for the town is not much more than a century old, there were excursions across the 18 miles of Wash. The lad, Fred Bloomfield, was uncertain whether he should accompany his young brother on that August morning in 1895, for it was a Sunday, and he was a chorister. In the end, he left home in a hurry, with a shoe unpolished, and the two boys boarded the "Princess of Wales", which set sail for Skegness. There were only 16 passengers aboard, though the vessel could accommodate 89; by 11 o'clock the voyage was nearly over, the Skegness pier only 1½ miles distant. Then it was that the skipper—Riches by name—saw the squall coming. The mast was lowered, and the skipper had the presence of mind to cut adrift a rowing boat in tow. Then the ship was struck by the full force of the wind and overturned.

When the skipper came to the surface five passengers were clinging to him; he was unable to swim with them all, and disengaged himself from two. With the remainder he reached the rowing boat, and got them in it. After that Riches saved 8 others, but all were in a precarious position, only keeping afloat by baling. In the nick of time, a steam trawler came to the rescue, and the survivors were landed at Boston in the evening.

About 3 o'clock on that Sunday, the Hunstanton Coastguards received a message by the telegraph; "Pleasure boat from Hunstanton sunk, all on board taken off." After that the telegraph station closed, and anxious people were kept in suspense till Monday, when the noon railway train brought in the survivors. Five had perished, including that promising lad, Fred Bloomfield, but his younger brother was safe.

In spite of this disaster, excursions across the Wash continued till the first World War. Now, pleasure boats go only as far as the sandbank, from which seals slip off into the water, though the intrepid have made the crossing of the Wash on water-skis.

Hunstanton cliffs present a remarkable sandwich of colours. The top layer is white chalk, then there is a seam of red chalk, and the base is ginger-brown carrstone, from which so many houses in the town were built. To northward on the shore was the Oyster Sea, remarked upon in old guide books. There in season "are caught skate, oysters, lobsters, bredcock, soles, maids, plaice, salmon, trout, and hornpikes". At the turn of the century a present Hunstanton resident went fishing in the oyster sea for crabs, shrimps, etc. Then a fisherman laid a mussel bed there, but he died before it matured.

Early inquisitive visitors to Hunstanton walked along the sands till they "arrived at the prostrate forest, consisting of numberless large timber trees, many of them decomposed, and so soft that they might easily be penetrated with a spade." For hereabouts, some 4000 years ago, was a great forest with many oak trees, stretching out far from the present shore, and frequented by people with flint implements.

The first guide book, which appeared about 1864, describes New Hunstanton (for the separate old village to the north had existed since time immemorial) as a "group of houses scarcely worthy of designation more exalted than that of a hamlet." By 1865 it possessed "about 30 commodious lodgings and boarding houses, and there are three first-class hotels . . . 20 bathing machines and several pleasure boats. In 1873 it had reached the status of a small town" with 800 inhabitants. The present population is 4000. It was not until 1894 that New Hunstanton, or Hunstanton St. Edmunds, became a separate parish, "now a well known and much frequented watering place", said to be noted for the absence of fogs, "in spring the east wind is less keen than in the Midland counties".

Hunstanton cliffs stand 60 ft. about the beach, and here was a beacon long ago, a guide to shipping in the dangerous waters, and a warning to trained bands inland of the approach of French and Flemish privateers bent on pillage. In the latter half of the 18th century a new lighthouse was built. The previous one cannot have been very helpful, "seamen were sometimes obliged to awaken the old gentleman with a shot to put him in mind that his fire wanted blowing". The present lighthouse has not been used for many years, since the Lynn Well light vessel took over, and is now a private residence.

Near to the lighthouse is the traditional site of the landing of Edmund from Germany in the 9th century, who was crowned King of East Anglia, and afterwards martyred.

53

The remains of a ruined chapel may mark the site of a rough building in which the saint-king is said to have dwelt for the best part of a year in order to learn the Book of Psalms by heart in the Saxon tongue.

Hunstanton is one of those Norfolk place-names in which the middle syllable is not sounded, and the way to say it is "Hunstan". Upon a fine summer Sunday the esplanade and beach at New Hunstanton are crowded with happy holiday folk from Midland towns, and a marching band makes martial music. The flat sea supports blue sails and speed-boats. Some predict that the salt waters of the Wash will become a fresh water lake, protected by a huge dam, or, perhaps, the site of a new town. But back in 1837 others dreamed of draining the great inlet, making it into a good habitable place, and calling it after the young Queen, Victoria County.

Two miles inland from Hunstanton there is no crowd in the steep, turf-clothed valley of Ringstead Downs. On the way there are the scant ruins of Barret Ringstead church, a depopulated village, now united with Hunstanton. Years ago the chalybeate spring in the valley was "extensively recommended by the faculty" to visitors. Few penetrate there now ; the secluded cleft remains a place out of a dream.

RUNTON HALF-YEAR LAND

IN THE height of the summer season the coast road through the Runtons may be too busy to please the peace-loving stranger. The village streets present, perhaps, but small attraction to the connoisseur of the rural scene, though should he penetrate inland he will find pleasant and quiet commons, and behind them a bracken and gorse-clothed ridge. On the cliff side of the main road are hundreds of caravans. But should he come here again after the middle of October, he will notice a change ; the caravans have all disappeared, and there is green sward to the abrupt edge of the cliffs. Here are nine hundred acres of Half-Year Land which covers not only the seaward side of the road but extends inland to the ridge. This is a "museum piece" left over from the middle ages, exhibiting ancient agricultural methods.

So, for hundreds of years, the people of East and West Runton have had the right to feed sheep on Half-Year Land between October 11th, Old Michaelmas Day, and April 6th, Old Lady Day. During that time all gates and hindrances should be removed. No Enclosure Act has extinguished this privilege, and it remains the delight of many and the disgust of some. No houses may be built on Half-Year Land, though a number have intruded by one means or another, and the railway has penetrated it. However, a great deal of land remains unsullied by modern masonry.

There is now a communal flock belonging to the Runtons, and a larger one existed within living memory. The last shepherd of it retired in 1912. His wages were paid by the owners of sheep in proportion to the number contributed. Latterly, the shepherd received about 12/6 per week ; also he could claim 6d for every lamb born, and 2/6 for leaving the flock over night on private land, for purposes of manuring. Rules for the inclusion of sheep in the flock were strict, and no animal which had been taken out of the parish for a night could be returned. After the sheep had had their fill on the Half-Year Land, cloven-footed animals could be turned out in the day-time, and later the cloven-foot qualification was relaxed, and ponies and donkey were allowed.

The Runton sheep were not the only flock which fed on the Half-Year Land. That of Beeston Priory Farm had the

55

right to the "first bite". Orginally this privilege belonged to the Priory of Austin Canons at Beeston-on-Sea, which was founded in the reign of King John. Ruins of it still remain to-day, grey and tattered against the green background. Sir William Paston was one of a commission of four men which inquired into the affairs of the Priory before its dissolution. There were then six canons who were "goode men", and there were also seven servants and six children. Probably there had been more canons once, judging from the size of the buildings. The Priory was dissolved in 1539; the Prior received a pension, and later he became Rector of Newton Flotman.

In summer when the Half-Year Land was evacuated by the sheep, it was used for communal cropping. The strips of individual parishioners were marked off by raised grass ridges, or baulks. Originally crops had to be harvested by Old Michaelmas Day, but in later times concessions seem to have been made to the growers of roots. If fenced at the owners' expense, and paid for at the rate of 6d. per acre, they were allowed to remain after the flock was turned out. Some of the old turf baulks are still visible, running straight across the green sward where now the caravans stand in summer-time.

At the beginning of this century the bounds of the Half-Year Land was perambulated annually, and a parishioner of East Runton remembers taking part in these exercises when she was a child. It seemed a long walk to her from the north-west boundary point, inland to the rough slopes of the ridge, by Icleborough Hill, Davy Hill, to Muckle Hill, near the Cromer bounds. But on Davy Hill they were refreshed with buns and oranges. A man accompanied the party steering bicycle wheels on handles, with an instrument attached for measuring the distance.

There is very little Half-Year Land left in England to-day, and no more in Norfolk, though some may have survived at Tacolneston into this century. The people of Runton have been zealous to preserve theirs from encroachment. Whatever its inconvenience, its existence helps in conservation of the coastal scenery.

SCOLT HEAD

ABOUT the last place in Britain Victorians of the '70's would have visited for enjoyment was Scolt Head, between Brancaster and Burnham Overy, called locally the Island, for the desolation would have moved them unpleasantly, the mud appalled them, and the uncouth shore offended their sense of the picturesque. Occasionally birdwatchers, wildfowlers, and botanists went to the place, and of course the natives visited it for various utilitarian purposes. In the Great War terns' eggs were used for food, and in less austere times boys delighted to go "perling"—collecting eggs and bombarding each other with them. But before the first quarter of this century had gone by, the place became quite fashionable, and an early party of visitors came bearing alpen-stocks to scale the sandhills! In 1923 the National Trust bought a large part of Scolt Head, and later the Nature Conservancy took it over on a 99 year lease.

When Alice first saw the dunes of the Island from Brancaster beach she was enthralled, for she was young enough to have seen very few hills of any sort. She was told it was no good trying to get there because the intervening channel was too deep to paddle through. Moreover, it was a dangerous place, maybe there were quicksands, at any rate the tide came rushing in and drowned the unwary, which details only added fuel to the child's desire to visit this lovely and mysterious island. At length desire was satisfied ; a fisherman took Alice and her mother by boat from Brancaster Staithe on the last of the tide, and fetched them when it began to flow again. Memory does not retain the details of that expedition, but the boatman, possibly thinking that if they were crazy enough to make it at all they might as well pay him handsomely, asked for the then prodigious sum of £1.

Many years later, when Alice had become quite an old woman, chance brought her to Brancaster beach. The tide was out, and the dunes of the Island drew her steps to the eastward, as they had done so long ago. The shore was as empty as ever, the powdery sand blew about in low swirls, cloud shadows moved over the great yellow expanse. It seemed a very long way to the channel, but her companion's legs gave out first, and they sat down amongst the dunes to the landward side of the beach. Here it was suddenly quiet and hot ; the sound of the sea was hushed, the air calm, and pale yellow hawk weed contrasted with the herbage. But Alice could not rest long, for the high dunes of the Island were beckoning to her. "I will just walk over there as far as that yacht", she said. The yacht was a large blue-and-white one, stranded on a pale sandbank. Three little boys were making castles by it, they stared at Alice, who walked on to a low full of water. She paddled through, touching an orange buoy which was made of plastic. How things had changed ! Then she reached the main channel separating the beach from the Island. The water looked deep ; as Alice hesitated, a solitary man in bathing trunks waded across to a willowy pole protruding from the channel near the opposite side. Alice forgot caution, she hitched up her skirt and went in. The water was up to the top of her thighs, but she got across, and was soon among the dunes, dragging a rheumatic leg up the steep ascent. But from the top the view to seaward was blocked by other heights. There was the great 60 ft. dune, and the Watcher's house nestling discreetly into the background, and a line of washing blew out behind it. Far away over the enormous scene to the landward side were two figures. Perhaps they were picking samphire—the poor man's asparagus.

Alice did not tarry long, but slid down the dunes, the easiest way to descend. The mud was sprinkled with sea birds feeding, and to the westward was a low tip of the Island. The tide was still ebbing, so Alice thought, and she began walking towards the spit, sinking ankle deep in mud. Then it was that the sole came off one of her old shoes, so she had to discard it, and the sharp shells made walking painful. It was just as well she turned back, for on reaching the channel the water appeared deeper. Alice went in, but sharp things at the bottom pricked her bare foot. She all but toppled over, and thought what an ass she was to venture alone at her age, in such a place. She floundered on through the deep water, and then, thankfully she reached the opposite side. She got to the sand castles by the yacht ; they would soon be flat on the bed of the ocean, and the yacht, tilted now on its side, would be upright and buoyant. The boys were nowhere to be seen.

Alice retraced her steps towards the sandhills behind the beach, and sat down, glad to rest her legs. Her companion and a fisherman were talking together. The latter turned to Alice, "Dangerous place you was in", he said, "tide 's beginning to flow". Alice walked back to her car to the landward side of the dunes, on the edge of the golf links, where the greens looked like velvet.

58

SMOKERS HOLE AND POND HILLS

LESS than a mile and a half from the busy little town, which is thronged with people from the villages on a Saturday afternoon, and the sides of the Street are stiff with cars, is that secluded spot called Smokers Hole. Once there were two ways of approach—down the common land, by a bridge over the stream, or by a well-worn path, in a fold of heath, leading off the main Norwich road. Both paths brought one to the long meadow, sheltered on the north by the slopes of the Common, and on the south by rising woods and fields. Here was a cottage by the bridge. In it lived a family of children, but the meadow was also a playground for many from the town. It was not strictly public property, but nobody was turned off. Men went there fishing, some tickled trout, children paddled or even bathed by the bridge. Boys from the Grammar School blocked the flow of the stream, and increased the depth, for their steeplechases.

Here, too, came sheep, to be dipped, each frightened animal being thrust in to emerge in a rush on the other side. The place was full of excitements. There were brown butterflies about ; one could gather water-cress or water-lilies, amid an overall scent of water-mint. Years before there had been a mill here ; even modern ordnance maps mark the cottage "Mill House" and show "Mill Lane". Faden's map of 1798 calls the stream "The Hempstead Beck", not the Glaven, by which name it is now dignified. Last century, Volunteers came to practise shooting here, and lay down in their scarlet and blue uniforms on the damp grass.

Later on the cottage was occupied by a widow called Long Sal. She had a dog which barked wildly when anybody was nigh, and a pony which she harnessed to a high cart, and drove up to the town once or twice a week.

"That may be a bit lonely, but that's home when you get back", said Long Sal. She had also a gander, which had been a pet, and had been given to her so that it might live out its old age in that highly suitable spot. "When I go for a bit o' kindling, he come an' all", said Sal, "and that's not a bit o' good hushin' him back, acause he don't pay no regard." But some time after that, she was callous enough to contemplate making a meal of the bird. In this she was disappointed, for though she boiled the carcase for hours, the flesh remained tough as leather. Long Sal had a son, who went away to serve as a soldier in the Great War, "A long way off, yin side o' Norwich."

At length total war penetrated even Smokers Hole. There were soldiers on the Common, practising with nefarious weapons. Loud explosions sounded in the valley ; the walls of the cottage trembled. Woods were falling flat, as trees were felled for the nation's need. There was sorry desolation abroad.

Then, one November day, Long Sal saw an officer approaching, with a paper in his hand. He told her it was no longer safe to stay in Smokers Hole, and she must go elsewhere. So the widow got together her few belongings, and someone "moved" her to Baconsthorpe, where she had a good house in the village. But she was not happy there, she longed for the freedom and quiet of her old home, to which she never returned.

*   *   *   *   *

More than twenty years passed, and Smokers Hole was almost a forgotten place, no longer visited by company from the town. The path over the Common had disappeared in a tangle of birch thicket, and the opening to the path on the Norwich road was concealed by a growth of young conifers. Suspecting that the way to Smokers Hole was altogether grown over with bracken and heather, I put on my slush boots for protection against adders, and began struggling through trees and undergrowth. Suddenly the old well-worn path, along which Long Sal had driven her pony and cart, opened up before me. In its old style, it ran downwards to the little wood at the bottom of the valley, where some cypresses had been planted, an incongruous sight in that well-remembered setting.

The gate beyond the wood was padlocked. Inside the meadow some electric pylons strode across the meadow. There had been cattle here, and someone had been cutting the rough herbage into swaithes. The stream flowed between clean cut banks ; there were no water-lilies, no water-cress, but a single brown butterfly was on the wing. The ruins of the cottage were almost hidden by undergrowth, and the fruit trees behind were naked and dead. Smokers Hole was no longer a home and a pleasure ground, but a place of sombre utility. It must not be idle longer, but made to take a part in the economic scheme. Change in the country is so often for the worse, but memory survives change ; shut the eyes, and there is the delicious meadow, full as ever with life and colour and enchantment.

In a more sophisticated county the signpost would have "Pond Hills" upon it, but here it bears only the name of the next village, which lies upon the main road. In a more uneven part of England, the term "Hills" might not be applied to the low undulating wooded ridge. Yet, in its modest way, Pond Hills is a famous place locally. During the 1939-45 war, when an invasion seemed likely, it was a top secret that the way of escape for refugees was along the winding lane through the woods, which was so humble that the armed forces could do without it. At all times, it is a useful route across country, for anybody who knows how to find it.

"Don't you go throu' Pond Hills, do you 'ont get there," the motorist may be warned in winter time, for if there have been snowdrifts they are sure to linger in the lane long after other roads are clear. But if even winter tarries, the sweets of spring are here in abundance, and it is not only for being a convenient short cut that this very minor road is so esteemed, but because it gives access to a local Eden.

About Easter, people begin straying into the woods. The Keeper, who is guardian of the place, and lives in a cottage by the Pond, has a dog which barks incessantly when intruders are around. It must be irritating to endure that din ; the poor man emerges from the trees shouting at three little girls who have gathered pussy willow. "They think they can go anywhere", he grumbles, oblivious, apparently, that I have just come from another part of the wood. But there is no stopping people when primroses are in flower. Folk have been gathering them time out of mind, and they do no harm. The first person to espy the flowers is the woman who rides her bicycle through Pond Hills to work. "There 's a sight o' primroses in that there plantin", she declares. "You want to find the bit o' wood I've left by the wire fence, then you can set your foot on it and get over nicely". At the farther end of Pond Hills, the trees were felled during the war, and the place replanted. Here, on the warm western slope, are primroses of the best. They are long-stalked and faintly scented, and in the intoxication of picking them, one cannot stop. Here are anemones too, frail fairy flowers ; bringing them indoors seems unkind.

By the week-end, tidings of the primroses have spread. "Saveral" people are here, and some have come from far away. The Keeper stands by the fence watching them, and chatting quite affably. The Truce of the Primrose is on. Flowers will be carried back to many homes ; they will serve to trim up churches, and be put in jam jars on graves.

Nobody seems to object to wanderers on the low meadows, which lie in the shallow valley between the hills. They go

61

on and on, luring footsteps to farther solitudes, and distant thickets. The little stream from the Pond slips through the midst of them, and it is boggy about it, but higher up the turf is short and dry. Under the shelter of the flowering blackthorn (which the superstitious will not pick) is a bower of sunbeams, warm enough to bask in. There is a scent of violets, and suddenly the chiff-chaff starts calling. Soon it will be the cuckoo, shouting faintly from afar, to say he has come back.

Later on come the bluebells. In a flood of cool colour, they sweep through the trees, causing the passer-by to stop and drench his eyes with them. Bluebells are not flowers to pick ; children, of course, try to carry away their elusive beauty, but a bunch of bluebells, with trailing white stems, is a pathetic sight.

When the bluebells have faded, the season of Pond Hills is over. People pass along the lane on their lawful occasions, but they do not dally long, even in the shade of the mid-summer trees, and the Keeper's dog gets a rest.

THE SEVEN BURNHAMS

"IT IS a fine open champaign country bordering upon the sea. On the descent from Docking to the Burnhams is a remarkably fine landscape ; the several towns of Burnham, interspersed below with a view of Mr. Wilkinson's house, and an extensive prospect of the British ocean, form together to the mind a *coup d'aeil* truly delightful and striking". So wrote a traveller some 200 years ago.

The seven Burnhams are Westgate, Sutton, Norton, Ulph, Overy, Deepdale, and Thorpe. But now Westgate, Sutton, and Ulph, have united into the one parish of Burnham Market. Parson Woodforde thought it "a very pretty Country Town". After partaking of cheese, butter, and porter at Wells, he had come a "very pleasant ride all by the Sea, and by Holkham House, Mr. Coke's". He stayed the night at the Pitts' Arms Inn at Burnham Market, "a rider supped and spent the Evening with me". Doubtless the inn got its name because Lord Camelford, cousin of the Prime Minister (the Younger Pitt) had made a lucrative match with the daughter of Pinckney Wilkinson, who had built and lived at the big house near Westgate Green and church.

To-day, Burnham Market is still a pleasant place ; amongst the old houses facing each other across the green is not one intruder from a less seemly age. Through the midst of the plain goes the Goosebeck channel, dry as a bone at present. "That wont flow this year", said a woman "because that did two seasons ago, and that only comes once in seven years." Mr. Wilkinson's house, "a very elegant seat" is now a home for the elderly. At the opposite end of the town is All Saints church of Ulph, with a bell-turret, and a rather gloomy interior. As for St. Ethelbert's of Sutton (commonly called St. Albert's) it is but a ruin overflowed with ivy.

"London, York, and Coventry, and the Seven Burnhams by the Sea", an old saying, is obscure. The present total population of all the Burnhams is approximately 2000. True, there is sometimes a market on Westgate Green, when there are enough odds and ends to warrant it, and quantities of malt were once produced in the neighbourhood for London brewers, and carried away by ship from Burnham Overy Staithe.

Overy Staithe is quite a lively place still in the summer, when people come from far and wide for sailing. Up to the beginning of this century small ships still called to fetch malt. In 1845 there was considerable activity. A Harbour Master reigned at the Staithe, and pilots in small boats went out to "kedge" incoming traffic up the creek. Ships were from 60 to 80 tons, and trade was carried on in corn, coal, malt, and oysters. Of the latter there was "an excellent bed in the offing, where 5 boats and 15 fishermen are regularly employed."

The land of the Burnhams received temperate praise from a Victorian. "The country round is agreeably diversified with hill and dale, and the air is highly salubrious . . . It is terminated by an insulated ridge of sand-hills called Scalds Head, occupied only by rabbits". Little did the writer suspect how notable Scolt Head was to become as a nature reserve !

The little river Burn flows across the marshes to join the Overy creek after it has surged through the mill which belongs now to the National Trust. But before it was built, ships ascended as far as the upper mill, in Overy Town. Overy Staithe and Overy Town form the parish of Burnham Overy. The Town, in spite of its high-sounding name is made up of a few decent flint houses near the ancient church, with its low central tower, which is settled comfortably into a hillock above the road. The round steeple of Burnham Norton church shows up on the rising fields ; not far away is the gateway to the former priory of Carmelite Friars, which was founded in the thirteenth century. A short time before it was dissolved by Henry VIII, only four friars remained, who were too poor to pay for repairs to their house, so were willing to part with it. A minor road trails northward to Burnham Norton Street, which goes down to the marsh. Upon a fine summer day here is the serenity of the edge of the world. Flowers bloom in gateways and above old walls. Beyond is the marsh, softly mauve with sea lavender, spreading away in an August dream to the sand-hills and the ultimate blue.

Burnham Deepdale, the most westerly Burnham, has a background of marsh but stands by the busy coast road. Noisy cars pass the humble church with its round tower, off which the lead was stripped, like so much paper, by a winter gale. Inside the building is a Norman font, around which figures in relief depict the revolving seasons.

Burnham Thorpe is the most easterly of the seven Burn-hams, and the farthest inland. Its fine thick houses stand by the Burn stream, which, like the Goosebeck, has a habit of disappearing for months at a stretch by sinking through the gravel. Here, at the old parsonage, which has long ago been pulled down, lived Horatio Nelson, an ailing boy who suffered from the ague "which was at that time one of the most common diseases". Here, too, he came when he was fretting on half-pay ; he coursed with Coke's harriers, bird-nested with his wife, and shot partridges alone as "he let fly without ever putting the fowling-piece to his shoulder."

Inhabitants of the Burnhams were guilty of characteristic and homely misdemeanours six centuries ago. The lord of the manor ordered John Mann and William Gunn to relinquish the tunic, boots, and socks, which they had taken from a body cast up from a wreck. John Gunn took also rabbits from the lord's warren with ferrets and hooks. People got into trouble for "keeping dangerous dogs given to biting men." John King was fined for keeping two bulls "which destroy the corn of different people and rush at men with their horns". Lastly, Robert, son of Edward Palle, was fined 6d. for "standing at night under the windows of John Gasele to hear the secrets of the said John."

THURNING (or Thirning)

THERE is a lot said these days about dormitory villages and dying villages, but if, indeed, the latter are going to disappear, there is a kick in some of them yet, and many are pleasant parishes. What they lack in modern conveniences is made up for in neighbourliness. Each Norfolk village contributes its individuality to the scene. The scattered houses of Thurning (or Thirning) are linked by very narrow twisting roads, none of them marked "A" or "B". Thurning means "the place where thorns grow", and in the last 1000 years great events have passed it by. It lies 5 miles north of Reepham, $1\frac{1}{2}$ from Wood Dalling, and 2 from Briston, but the houses are so scattered that it is confusing to talk about exact mileages. There are 31 houses in Thurning, 8 of which are empty, and the parish has a population of 68 ; at the beginning of the century there were 160 inhabitants.

Thurning has electricity but no main drainage, no post office, or public call box, no Council Houses, no school, no pub, and the nearest shop is at Wood Dalling. But, "Thirning is a good place to live in", remarked an inhabitant, "anybody 'll lend a hand to help ye. There's a new feller come to live in the bottom house, and he like it well 'enou'." The young man in Wood Dalling Shop wears a smart linen jacket, and would put many town assistants to shame. "We send down the orders to Thurning", he said. "I like these villages myself, born and bred here I was. That's proper country, and mightn't suit folk from towns". The "Green Man" at Briston is not too far away for people to give each other lifts. Some children attend Briston school ; they are not snatched up by coach, and taken to some far foreign atmosphere.

Many of the men in Thurning work on farms, and everybody knows everyone. Only the great gash for the sea-gas pipe, just beyond the parish boundary, reminds one of the feverish and ugly hustle of to-day. A beck flows diagonally across the middle of Thurning, and another passes to the south making a dividing line with Wood Dalling ; nearly all the buildings keep to higher ground.

The "Rookery" is a handsome farmhouse (there are two others). Nearby is a line of cottages with plentiful gardens before them ; the broad old roofs sweep down low over the windows, the whole providing an air of perfect tranquility.

The weather-beaten church is 14th century. The Rectory was built in 1829, and has no nonsense about it, but here, in the shrubbery, come up thousands of aconites and snowdrops. The Hall shows from the trees above a little lake. In 1865 it was considered "a handsome mansion which has been much improved". Perhaps, on the whole, it was more pleasing when the Elwin family lived there, and it was caught up in Parson Woodforde's world. For Mrs. Davy was a sprightly widow, and she and her daughter were friends of Woodforde and his niece Nancy. On a December day in 1785, the first pair "went in the Lenwade Bridge Chaise for Thurning . . . to one Mr. Elwins, there to enter their new boarding place. Mrs. Davy was very low indeed at going away." The Elwins were "very good creditable people and genteel. Mr. Thomas Elwin appears to be a very worthy man, a married man with 4 or 5 children. Every person who knows him speaks well of him." This Mr. Elwin was grandfather of the Rev. Whitwell Elwin, rector of Booton ; from that remote retreat, he edited the *Quarterly Review* from 1853-60. The Elwins left Thurning about the middle of the last century, and the Gay family came to live at the Hall. James Gay belonged to the republican movement which resulted from dislike of the Prince Consort, and Queen Victoria's long retirement after his death. The movement was strong in Norwich.

About this period, that self-important body, the Fakenham and Dereham Archery Club, held meetings, which included luncheon and afternoon tea, at the homes of various members. At lunch it was customary to drink the Queen's health, and as James Gay objected to this, the Club would not shoot on his ground. After his death, his grandson, and then his grand-daughters lived on at Thurning Hall till the 1930s, and the archers met regularly there every summer. For the Republicans had faded away in the triumphant closing years of the old Queen's reign. Inside the house there was dark wall paper, heavy curtains with tasselled cords, and thin china tea cups on the mahogany table. Miss Rose Gay, then an old woman, had an unorthodox style of shooting, but her arrows were often piercing the gold on the target. She was very kind and sympathetic to young archers (who were warned not to imitate her shooting !) The Misses Gay bought a motor car, and their fat old coachman turned into a chauffeur. He drove along the twisting roads at speed, but the sisters did not care, for they were so unused to motors that they failed to realise what a menace they were to others and themselves. When the second war came, the sisters were dead, and Thurning Hall became a Land Army Hostel.

Rose Gay would have been surprised at the goings-on, but would not have been shocked, perhaps.

Mary Long, unlike the Misses Gay, did not have a sheltered or easy life. A fragment of her history is left, and it throws a glimmer of life on forgotten days. In 1798, at the age of eleven, being one of a large family, her father applied to the Overseer of the Poor at Thurning for help. Mary was taken from home and placed as Town Girl (a servant) with Mrs. Dont, a farmer's wife. She continued working for various mistresses till she was about fifteen, when she was informed that Mrs. Parslee of Holt (6 miles away) wanted a servant, so she "Let herself from that time (Lady Day) to the following Michaelmas at Half a Guinea Wages and her Board". There she stayed for 18 months, her pay being raised to 30/-, which Mrs. Parslee gave her in clothes and money. This was an important situation for Mary's future, for by working as a "yearly servant" for a full year she gained a "settlement" at Holt instead of Thurning, which meant that the former parish would have to support her in case of need. About 2 years afterwards, she was working for a Mrs. Plaford of Wood Dalling, when, about a fortnight before Christmas, she had to leave, "not being able to do the whole of her work, her Mistress and she parted by mutual consent". After that, we do not know what became of her ; maybe she suffered from poor health and stayed with her family at Thurning. But in September 1808, she was pregnant, and as she now "belonged" to Holt, thither she was moved, and put into the workhouse on the heath. There we lose sight of Mary Long, but she had to tell her life-story before a magistrate, in case there was any doubt as to which parish she belonged. Thus, by chance, her identity is preserved as a long-past inhabitant of Thurning.

Section Three
PASTIMES IN NORFOLK

A Game of Bowls

ARCHERY

ARCHERY was always respectable, in fact for many generations the Law decreed that every man must practise it upon a Sunday. At Archery the Englishman was supreme, and bows and arrows were far more effective in battle than early firearms. It was revived as a pastime (never a game, one "shoots" at archery, never "plays" !) about the 'forties of the last century.

Mr. R. J. H. Harvey, M.P., of Crown Point, Whitlingham, was at a loss to imagine why he should have been chosen president of the Norwich Archery Society, as he had never shot with a common bow, trusted he did not draw a long one, and it was many years since he had used the little blind boy's either ! In the summer of 1866, the Grand National Meeting of the United Kingdom was held in his grounds, and 74 male and 72 female archers assembled at the targets.

It was a dull, still day, and there were not a great number of spectators. "It may be", someone suggested, "that so polite an art and elegant a pastime is scarcely adapted to the members of a great mercantile community." Yet the scene was certainly picturesque. The 27 pairs of targets gave a fine splash of colour ; there was a marquee, and the bands of the Norfolk Light Horse and the Norwich Volunteer Artillery were grouped on either side of the ground ready to play selections alternately. To the north might be seen the pretty village of Thorpe, with laden wherries gliding along the river below, and to the west loomed the principal buildings of the City of Norwich.

Each day the gentlemen were to shoot the York Round of six dozen arrows at 80 yards, and 100 yards, 4 dozen arrows at 80 yards, and 2 dozen at 60 yards. These were "the Prince's lengths", favoured by the Prince of Wales when he shot with the Royal Toxophilite Society in the 1780's. He was said also to have been responsible for the scoring of the target rings—nine for a gold, seven a red, five a blue, three a black, and one a white.

But it was the female archers who attracted the greatest interest. Having set aside the embroidery frame, they took up the bow and quiver to shoot the National Round of

4 dozen arrows at 60 yards, and 2 dozen at 50. "The most intelligent of onlookers could not but be thankful for any cause which could bring so fair a line of archers as that which appeared before him when the order to shoot was given. Indeed, the onlookers seemed utterly careless whether the arrows went into their mark or not, it was enough to watch the various graceful attitudes of the shooters."

For the archery was not so very good in spite of the absence of wind and dazzling sunshine which had soon dispersed the early morning cloud. Arrow after arrow went whirring past the targets, to the no small danger of onlookers. But one lady from Co. Dublin, "distinguished by a gold medal on her left breast, drew general attention, nearly all her arrows plunging into the painted surface with the thud that told of a skilful archer, and her graces gave double charm to her skill." Yet even her prowess was not such an attraction as the horticultural show in another part of the ground.

On the second afternoon of the meeting, rain began to fall smartly, but the ladies remained at the targets, the gentlemen gallantly supplying umbrellas. At 7 o'clock the shooting was over, and the bedraggled archers made a rush for the cabs and other vehicles to take them back to the city. The lady from Dublin was the champion winning a £20 prize. The third and last day was for the handicap events, for which several prizes were forthcoming from Norwich itself. Mr. Caley gave a shawl, Mr. Chamberlin a sealskin coat, Mr. Howlett a concertina. There was also a muff, a musical box, some ivory brushes, and Bohemian glasses.

The archers are dead and gone, though, maybe, the musical box, the ivory brushes, and the Norwich shawl, are somewhere to be found even now.

*   *   *   *   *

The Fakenham and Dereham Archery Club is not even of minor historic importance, but it lingered on into a new age, a museum piece in a very different England. In spite of its name the Club never seems to have shot at Fakenham, at least since 1894, but it met at various members' grounds in central Norfolk, and sometimes the archers went as far as Holt, Lammas, and Norwich.

On August 7th, 1914, Mr. and Mrs. C. "only shot the long, as they were anxious least their house should be taken for the War before they got home." After that, the Club did not shoot till 1920, and then with a reduced membership.

72

Meetings were fortnightly, from May to September. In the 1920's the countryside was very soothing to the casual observer, but not to the poorer inhabitants, for some farm labourers were getting only 30/- a week. Dilapidated buildings showed the depressed state of agriculture, dusty hedges with many trees, edged the cosy roads, and a "dickey cart" or horse and tumbrel was a usual sight. Near the biggest house in the village the targets were set up, either on a park or pasture. They had come by train to the nearest station four miles away, and the Secretary, who had arrived in the morning, and stayed to lunch, had seen to their erection.

About 2.30, the company arrived, some from considerable distances. Most of them were middle-aged or even old, with here and there a youngster to pick up dowagers' arrows. This was not so easy as it sounded ; the unwary might step upon an arrow and break it, or run the feathered end into the shin. Then some archers liked their arrows left where they fell, "Leave it alone, child !" Cattle which had been penned for the occasion, watched from behind the fence, till they lost interest in this apparently harmless pursuit. Once the Club Record Book recorded "the weather was extremely hot, and bow-strings stretched so much it was difficult to get up to the target." Old women, quivers strapped round the waist, shot surprisingly well ; younger and more graceful female archers were not nearly so expert. Any arrow hitting the gold circle in the centre of the target was measured by the Secretary, and it sometimes happened that a beginner got "the best gold".

After the shooting was over, the archers put back their arrows carefully into wooden boxes ; the beautiful wooden bows which were inlaid with mother-of-pearl, tipped with horn, and decorated with ribbons, went into green baize cases. Then there was tea ; how cool it was in that dark and dated dining-room ; The deep red curtains with mustard-coloured tassels, had hung there since the 'eighties. Nothing but oil lamps and candles had ever lighted that room.

The fireplace was an ornate Victorian affair, but the cups and saucers were of elegant old china. Not even the upheaval of world war had altered the appearance of that room ; the two old maiden sisters who owned it were unchanged by the changing times.

*   *   *   *   *

Driving home with her mother, the wholly unnecessary cotton rug over her knees, the youngest archer felt that she was awaking from a Victorian dream.

73

F

In these days when archery is a business-like affair, and steel bows have taken the place of the traditional wooden ones, there is tea in a canteen. But it is impossible not to look back with a certain regret to the less expert, but perhaps more civilised meetings of the Fakenham and Dereham Archery Club.

BOWLS

EVEN the harmless game of bowls was once frowned upon by the State, seemingly because it interfered with the practise of archery, which fostered the military spirit of the country. It is uncertain whether the game was first played outside on the grass, or under cover in alleys. The "throwing of stones" (ancient bowls) was included in the time of Edward III among "games alike dishonourable, useless, and unprofitable". Some years later, servants, artificers, and labourers, were forbidden to play it. In the next century, half-bowl was condemned among the "new imagined plays", which all classes followed "to their impoverishment . . . and by their ungracious procurement and encouraging to induce others to such plays till they are utterly undone."

Even murders and robberies were ascribed to bowls, so that it was forbidden, either in garden or house, under pain of fine and imprisonment. Though Henry VIII added bowling alleys to Whitehall, he was severe against the game outside. Magistrates were ordered to search out those who, for gain, kept places of bowling, but, strangely enough, no punishment followed conviction, except the binding-over of offenders in their own recognisances, and making them sureties not to break the law again. Servants and others might play at Christmas time in their master's house and presence, but nobody could at any time "play at any bowle or bowles in an open place out of his garden or orchard."

Drake was at bowls when the Armada was sighted, and Charles I was an enthusiast of the outdoor game. He played during captivity, and is said to have been on the green at Holmby House, Northamptonshire, when he was arrested by Cornet Joyce with 500 troopers at his back.

Common bowling alleys were not suppressed finally till the 18th century, but bowling greens increased, and became fashionable additions to country houses. A foreigner remarked of them, "They are so even that they bowl upon them as easily as on a great billiard table ; and, as this is the usual diversion of gentlemen in the country, they have thick rowling-stones to keep the green smooth". Parson Woodforde was at bowls on Mr. Du Quesne's green at East Tuddenham in 1784. There were three of them playing, and the Parson lost 6d. He had brought a cucumber in his pocket for his host. Afterwards, "we had a most gracious rain this evening, and it lasted." A pleasant country scene from the Shades of Time.

In the records of bowling in Norfolk in the last century, the *Norwich Mercury* relates how, on the last day of August, 1807, a match was played on the green at Cley-next-the-Sea, between gentlemen of Cley and three of Holt for 50 guineas a side. The Holt team won, but the result of the return match is unknown. The players of this part of Norfolk must have fancied themselves, for some years later six gentlemen of the neighbourhood issued a challenge in the Press to six others from any county for the sum of 50 guineas a side. We do not know whether the challenge was taken up.

The famous Bowling Green Hotel stood at the top of Theatre Street, Norwich. Here, in 1839, two handsome pieces of plate were bowled for by the subscribers. "A band will be in attendance, and no person will be admitted but by ticket, price 2s. 6d. each, for which a pint of wine will be given." It was on this very bowling green that George Borrow saw the bruisers of England assembled one July evening in 1820—Tom Cribb and the rest—before the great fight at North Walsham between Ned Painter and Tom Oliver.

By the beginning of the 'nineties there were about a dozen organised clubs in Norfolk and Suffolk, including North Walsham "Angel", Dereham "George", Dereham "King's Head", Kirkley "Marquis of Lorne", Lowestoft "Great Eastern", Fakenham "Lion", and Diss "Cherry Tree". Friendly matches were often played for teas, the losers paying. One of the oldest of Bowling greens, and one which is still used, is at Erpingham "Eagle".

*   *   *   *   *

"Where's George ? " "Why, I reckon he is on the bowling green", would be the reply any fine summer evening nowadays. For the place has an irresistible draw for middle-aged and older men. It has become a centre of the village, and because of it, folk forget parish meetings and other important engagements. Once on the green, they are oblivious to all else. Even the mist creeping in from the sea, with a bitter chill, only makes them put their hands in their pockets between times. The green shows pale in the dusk, but still they play on, while their wives sit comfortably by firesides (if indeed they have them in these cheerless days of central heating). Bowls is a man's game. Women may play it, but they don't look quite right.

CAMPING

SOMEBODY in 1780 wrote "The inhabitants of Norfolk are so much attached to the Sports of the field that the turf is not much encouraged . . . Cock-fighting (for the honour of Norfolk) is not much followed. Nor do we find any irrational exercise, if we except kemping and wrestling in practise."

When Queen Victoria was crowned, they played at camp-ball in the lane leading to Baconsthorpe Old Hall, and upon the great meadow before the house. The boy, Tom Potter, joined in the sport, being then 14 years of age. Far out-living the Queen, Tom used to speak to his children about that memorable day—of the roast beef and plum puddings with great lumps of suet in them, which glistened in the sunshine, but, unfortunately, he did not tell them much about the ancient game of camp-ball. For camp-ball, or camping, was a great game in the Eastern Counties, probably a parent of modern football.

> *"Get campers a ball*
> *To camp there withall."*

was a Norfolk couplet of the 15th century, and a dim memory of the game is preserved in field names, such as Camping Land, Camping Close, Camping Ground. There was a Camping Field abutting the churchyard at Swaffham, and others at East Bilney, Stiffkey, and elsewhere. At Felbrigg the sport was encouraged by William Wyndham, statesman and philosopher. He said it combined all athletics, that a player must be a good boxer, runner, and wrestler. By 1830 someone stated of camping that it was "an ancient athletic game at ball now almost superseded by cricket, a less hardy and dangerous sport." For camp-ball was certainly hardy, though there were two varieties—Rough-Play and Civil-Play.

Rules of camp-ball were elastic ; the number of players on each side was often 10 or 12, and the ground a hundred to two hundred yards long. Prizes were usual at matches, and included hats, gloves, shoes, and small sums of money. At the beginning of the game an "indifferent spectator" threw up a ball much the size of one used for cricket, and

77

"the contest for the ball begins, and never ends without black eyes and bloody noses, broken heads or shins, and sometimes serious mischief". He who got the ball ran with it towards his opponents goal, throwing to a confederate when hard pressed, for if caught with the ball he lost a "snotch" for his side. Thus camp-ball bore some resemblance to Rugby football. Sometimes a larger ball was used which could be kicked; the sport was then called kicking-camp, and if boots were worn, savage-camp. Boots were tipped with horn, hardened with blood.

In the parish of Ranworth there were several notable camping matches. One was in July 1822, between the Hundreds of Blofield and Tunstead and Happing. It was a glorious day, and the rutted roads leading to the remote marshland were thronged with carts, chaises, wagons, and caravans, with horsemen and foot passengers. For "the news of the resumption of an athletic sport for which Norfolk has been of old so famous, has excited very great interest."

The camping-ground was roped in; thirty wagons placed lengthwise provided accommodation for the spectators, of whom there were about 4,000. Amongst them might have been seen an elderly female of the Blofield Hundred, urging her grandson to take part in the contest, and uphold the family reputation for camping, which it had held for the best part of a century. Nothing loath, the youth threw off his upper garments, and joined the players, "all fine young men in excellent health and spirits". Each of them was attended by his second, and play was to last for half an hour only. Blofield gained the first goal, and soon after the other side scored. "At one time the whole twenty were paired off, striving one against the other for victory, and so closely were the men matched for strength, courage, skill, and activity, the ball was nearly in the centre of the ground, when, the time being up, the play stopped, nor was it possible in the power of anyone to say which side could have won." And, "the old campers of the County declared that they had never witnessed so manly and brave a contest." So the umpires divided the prize of £7 amongst all players.

In 1806, a match was arranged between the Hundreds of Blofield and Taverham. The Blofield men failed to turn up, so those from Taverham walked off with the prize of a hat apiece. Six days before Waterloo there was another memorable camping match at Ranworth, with 24 a side. A crowd of two or three thousand people was drawn thither to watch the sport, but no goals were scored, and the game was decided by a bye. At that time, a reader having opened his *Norwich Mercury* read "All eyes are upon the hostile armies and, as the moment of onset draws nigh, the anxiety of the nations which surround the combatants . . . becomes greater . . . What we really know of the numbers, appointment, description . . . of the forces on either side amounts to very little. The silence of such an interval, so like the dead of night which proceeds a battle, may well invite the contemplation of the chances by which we live or die . . . It seems as if the world had sent forth its whole array to decide the strife at once." Fortunately the issue of the battle was more decisive than that of the camping match at Ranworth.

Campers were supposed to be uniformly dressed in light flannel jackets, distinguished by colours ; whether they were generally so attired is doubtful, but certainly camping was a very rough and dangerous sport. There was an old man of Ellingham, called Rooshy Buller, who had played in a match at Ranworth, having walked all Saturday night to get there. He still bore the scars of bygone games, for each man singled out an opponent, and fought with boot and fist.

There is record of a "Grand Camping Match" between Norfolk and Suffolk in 1818. It is described as "the first thorough boxing camping match which has taken place for the last 35 years . . . it was astonishing to observe the spirit of gallantry which animated both parties". But these Grand Camping Matches were uncommon events compared to the games which were held in many Norfolk villages. Upon a Sunday afternoon the young men went out to the camping ground, where the grass was soft and slippery. Goals were marked by bushes, posts, or heaps of clothes, and the play began. It was absorbing exercise, not always good tempered. The cries of the players pierced the silence of the Sunday afternoon. Perhaps they disturbed an earnest Sabbatarian, who came to rail at the young men. But his words fell upon unheeding ears, for folk had played at camp-ball upon that meadow time without memory. So the game continued until the players had had enough of it.

* * * * *

Football, in some form is the oldest and most popular of English games. For at least six centuries there have been balls thrown or kicked about this island in spite of disfavour of authority. By a proclamation of Edward II, the game was forbidden in the streets of London. "Forasmuch as there is a great noise in the city caused by hustling over large balls, from which many evils may arise which God

79

forbid ; we command and forbid on behalf of the king, on pain of imprisonment, such games to be used in the city in future."

As a rival to archery, and other warlike practises, the suppression of football was ordered by Edward III, but neither he nor his successors succeeded in getting rid of those tiresome balls. The game, as played by the Elizabethans, was dangerous, players being maimed and sometimes killed. The Puritans disliked football or camp-ball. One of them called Stubbs, who wrote "The Anatomie of Abuses in the Realme of England" believed the world was going to end in 1583. Amongst other convincing reasons for this belief, he mentioned "football playing and other devilish pastimes upon the Sabbath day". He described the game as "it may rather be called a friendlie kinde of fyghte than a play or recreation—a bloody and murthering practise, than a felowly sport or pastime. For dooth not every one lyee in waight for his adversarie, seeking to overcome him and picke him on his nose, though it be on hard stones."

It may have been partly due to Puritan disfavour, but from the second half of the 17th century the popularity of football declined. But it survived in some schools and districts in various forms, such as camp-ball in the eastern counties, and hurling in the west. (Hurling was the name later applied to a game resembling hockey.) A football match, old style, might be played in narrow streets, or in open country with the goals miles apart, the players varying in number from dozens to scores.

It was between 1850 and 1860 that the popularity of football began to revive. This revival was due largely to the influence of the schools. The period marks the birth of the game in its modern forms. One of the first recorded instances of football in Norfolk, as distinct from camp-ball, was in December, 1868, when a side called the Norwich Football Club played a match against the King Edward VI Grammar School.

Section Four
NORFOLK PEOPLE

A Corner of Fair Green, Diss, showing some Old Cottages and Brewery Premises
(about 1890) see page 125

A DUKE OF NORFOLK'S
HURRIED JOURNEY

FROM Norwich to Holland and back in the day is not
exceptionally fast travelling now, but some 280 years ago
such a journey was thought to be impossible, and the
assumption may have saved Henry Howard his head. The
story of this journey, which serves as a link between the
time of the Glorious Revolution and our own, was written
down in 1812. The writer had been told it 40 years before
by "a very intelligent and respectable old gentleman (of
Norwich) who appeared to give it full credit, which he
would not have done without very good reason."

In 1688, Henry Howard, sixth Duke of Norfolk, was
thirty-four. Unlike most of his family he had become a
Protestant, probably due to influence upon him when he
was at Cambridge University. Henry Howard and many
others were seriously alarmed at King James's attempts to
introduce the Popish religion ; but for three years he had
served James loyally, and had been made a Knight of the
Garter, and Lord Lieutenant of Norfolk. When James
went to open a new Roman Catholic Church in Whitehall,
the Duke, bearing the sword of State, stopped at the door.
"My lord of Norfolk, your father would have gone further",
said James. "Your Majesty's father would not have gone
so far", replied the Duke.

*   *   *   *   *

On an evening in late September, Henry Howard had a
party at his Norwich palace. It contained "a room on
purpose to dance in, very large, and having the bravest
hangings . . . His candlesticks, tongs, fire shovels were of
silver . . . we drank out of pure gold". This palace stood
between Charing Cross and the Wensum. Evelyn described
it in 1671 as "an old wretched building, and part of it,
newly built of brick, is very ill understood." The gay and
dissolute society of the Restoration was often entertained at
the Duke's palace. "A banquet was given every night, and
three coaches were employed to fetch ladies every afternoon ; the greatest of these would hold 14 persons, and
cost £500 without the harness, which cost three-score more.

On this particular night, the Duke had asked several Papists among his guests. He was impatient that his friends should depart; as soon as the last had gone, he mounted his horse, and attended by a groom, rode forth into the night. They went eastward, and stopped at the lonely farmhouse of a tenant, within sound of the sea. Here the groom was bidden wait with the horses whilst his master attended to some business. The Duke then hurried down to the shore and boarded a fast sailing ship. The wind being exceedingly favourable, in a few hours the coast of Holland was sighted.

Near the Hague, William, Prince of Orange, was mustering a great army—to fight Algerine pirates, so he said, but few believed him. As the Duke of Norfolk strode through the camp to the headquarters he must have been beset with doubts and fears. Reason urged him forward, for King James had proved himself unfit to rule. Yet, perhaps, he felt ashamed at his treachery, perhaps he called to mind the words he had written to his lawful king some years back: "I dare answer that the Prince of Orange nor none of his party has the least correspondence with this country." Then the Duke overheard someone in the camp say "there goes the Duke of Norfolk." An English soldier had recognised him.

Henry Howard never reached the headquarters after all, but hurried back to the shore. The wind had changed, and blew the ship back to England as fast as she had come. No sooner had the Duke landed on the Norfolk coast than he set off hot-foot to Norwich. On arrival, he sent out invitations to his guests of the previous evening. Papist and Protestant laughed and talked in the candlelight—the Duke seemed as gay and carefree as the others.

Before long James's spies in Holland had reported the rumour of the Duke's visit to that country. Whereupon James sent to Norwich to arrest the culprit. It was well for the Duke that he had taken the precaution of asking the same guests on those two successive nights; they all, including the Papists, who would hardly have connived with treachery, testified that the Duke was in Norwich upon the date in question. As nobody thought of the possibility of a journey to Holland and back in less than twenty-four hours, the Duke was allowed to go free.

*   *   *   *   *

About six weeks later, when the Prince of Orange had landed in the west of England, and James, in terror, had promised to convene a free Parliament, the Duke held a meeting at Norwich and urged the citizens to be loyal to James. Less than a week after this James having fled the country, the Duke was in Lynn, telling the townspeople "to support and defend the laws and liberties and the Protestant religion, since the coming of the Prince of Orange has given us the opportunity to declare for the defence of them." As Lord Lieutenant, he thereupon called out the militia, and "people generally put orange ribbons in their hats".

The Duke's palace in Norwich was partially demolished in 1711. Some of its out-buildings were being used as a particularly loathsome workhouse in 1806. Later there was an inn on the site called The Duke's Palace, but that has disappeared now too.

ARTHUR YOUNG'S
NORFOLK JOURNEY

ARTHUR YOUNG was no stranger to Norfolk when he made
his farmer's tour through the East of England nearly two
hundred years ago. He had been apprenticed to a merchant's
house in Lynn, but showed no aptitude for the business, and
his mother gave him the direction of an estate at Bradwell
Hall. When he was still under thirty he made his journeys
through the country, observing agricultural methods.

He entered Norfolk by way of Walpole St. Peter and St.
Andrew, in the tract of country known as Marshland. The
roads were numerous, very irregular, and disagreeable to
travel upon. He visited Runcton, and passed on to Massingham, where he was delighted with what he saw. "The
country before the great work done by marling and enclos-
ing was a wild sheep walk, but through the uncommon
spirit of many great farmers, it has advanced in value to
an amazing degree." At Weasenham he saw Mr. Billing's
fields of carrots, but about Sandringham his improving
eye observed tracts of sandy land, "which are applied at
present only to the feeding of rabbits."

So he came to Snettisham, where scenery and good
management had created a demi-paradise. In this sheltered
place, where even the weather was so mild that rosemary
bushes survived cold winters, lived Nicholas Styleman, who
had enclosed much land, but "in executing the idea he
planned the outline in so candid and charitable a manner,
that he kept as strict an eye to the interests of the poor
people as to his own . . . The comfort of living in such a
parish induces many to come and reside in it; if 20 new
cottages were built they would immediately be filled."

Young then proceeded north, past the two famous farms
of Summerfield and Sunderland, near Docking. From Burnham to Wells he "observed the crops in general better
than any I had seen in Norfolk". At Warham not only the
superior agriculture but the scenery arrested his attention,
for he had an eye for natural beauties.

"Some villages and churches scattered about the valley
all tend to make it cheerful, while the thick woods, which

crown the tops of several hills, and the groves which sink into the vale, throw a picturesque beauty over the scene that cannot fail to impress the spectator."

Stiffkey likewise delighted him. "The vale which is composed of the finest verdure, winds in a very beautiful manner out of a thicket of woody enclosures and returns at the other behind a projecting hill. An humble stream glides through it, and adds a cheerfulness which water alone can confer."

Again he was impressed with what was, possibly, a view near Bayfield. "In a sequestered valley shut out from the sea. The whole forms one of those half gloomy, yet not unpleasant scenes, in which Poussin delighted."

*   *   *   *   *

Young visited Melton Constable, where from a windmill near the Park there was a prodigious fine view of rich woodland finely intermixed with trees. The road from Sheringham to Holt disgusted him. "A flat disagreeable country, a black ling heath, or whin cover, but all quite capable of cultivation. Sheringham Cliff is a very high steep shore. It looks on one side full upon the sea, and on the other over various country abounding with irregularities of land." Between Holt and Aylsham the country was generally well cultivated, though farms were small.

So Young came to Norwich, which he notes, is one of the most considerable cities after London. "It stands on more ground than any other." The manufactories were crepes, camblets, damasks, satins, etc. He found the husbandry about Norwich to be generally good, and visited Earlham, (H)Ethel, Braconash, Bramerton, and Shotesham. Mr. Fellows, of the latter village, showed him plane trees, in low, moist situations, saying they grew much faster than poplar. At Bramerton he remarked that there were few sheep, and that it took 1½ acres to feed a cow in summer, about Norwich only an acre. A dairymaid could look after 20 to 30 cows.

*   *   *   *   *

Young then set off for Yarmouth, through the Hundred of Flegg, which, he had heard, was cultivated in the most complete manner. He found scarcely any meadow or pasture, the cows being fed on clover and rye-grass. The employment of the women and children was spinning wool. "All drink tea, and some thrice a day."

87

The traveller stopped at Ormesby. He reflected upon the condition of the county at the beginning of the eighteenth century, and of much of it only 30 years before. All the north-east and west, and part of the east was sheep walk, let from 6d. to 2s. an acre. The great improvement was due to enclosure without Parliamentary assistance, use of marl and clay, excellent courses of cropping, turnips well hoed, the culture of clover and rye-grass, long leases, and large farms. Young disliked absentee landlords, antiquated methods, wastes and commons.

From Ormesby Young went to Yarmouth, and then passed out of Norfolk at Beccles, into his native Suffolk. Afterwards he travelled in Ireland, and in France, on the eve of the Revolution, observing farming ways, and other things besides. Author of several books on agriculture, which were very popular and important publications, he became Secretary to the new Board of Agriculture.

In his latter years, Young became blind, and had an unsuccessful operation for cataract. He died, when nearly 80, in 1820. By that time agriculture was in a bad way; enclosure had ruined the peasantry of England and it is said Young regretted his earlier enthusiasm for it.

COKE OF NORFOLK

ON a September night in 1796 the Rev. Mr. James Woodforde, lying in his bed at Weston Longville, dreamt : "I was at an Entertainment given by Mr. Coke at his House, amongst other dishes was a Fawn roasted but cold, and plenty of Hares roasted and cold also." Thus, in the Parson's dream we hear of that remarkable person, Thomas William Coke of Holkham, Billy Coke of Norfolk. It was not strange that Woodforde should dream of dining with Coke, for he received an invitation to Holkham, a few years previously, to a ball and supper, in commemoration of the Glorious Revolution of 1688. Woodforde had declined, perhaps for political reasons, for Coke was a Whig. Another refusal came from the Rev. Mr. Edmund Nelson, Rector of Burnham Thorpe, and yet another from his son. "Captain Nelson's compliments to Mr. and Mrs. Coke, and is sorry it is not in his power to accept their invitation for November 5th." The entertainment was a magnificent affair, but posterity would appreciate it more had Parson Woodforde attended.

In 1788, Thomas William Coke was a handsome man of thirty-four, who was making a name for himself in Parliament and had begun his career as an agriculturalist. He had inherited his estate from his maternal great uncle, Thomas Coke, Earl of Leicester, and his father had taken the name Coke. Young Coke had, in the year 1776, entered Parliament, as a Knight of the Shire for Norfolk, and at that time was the youngest member of the House ; in 1832, he was the oldest. Very soon Coke began to make his personality felt in politics. "To fear God, to help man, and to hate all Tories", these were his principles. In a corrupt age he was incorruptible, devoid of political ambition, and an upholder of civil and religious freedom. But he was no orator ; a contemporary remarked "In the imperfect relics of his speeches, the bones of a giant are discoverable."

Coke soon became acquainted with Fox, to whom he remained a lifelong friend. He was opposed to the war with the American colonists, whose rights and grievances appealed to his sense of justice ; it was he who brought forward the motion in Parliament that the independence of America should be recognised. The House divided, and there were 177 noes, and 178 ayes. Coke took the address to the King, to the horror of the Court wearing his ordinary country clothes, which was, however, the privilege of Knights of the Shire, though seldom exercised. Very handsome he looked in his long-tailed coat, leather breeches, top boots, and spurs. George III, loath to give up the American colonies, never forgave Coke for this act, but Coke cared for no man's opinion, neither had he any respect for senseless privilege. In those days Royalty alone was accustomed to drive six horses in town. There is a tale that Coke drove past the King's palace with five horses and a donkey as leader.

At the election of 1784, Coke had lost his seat. Parson Woodforde mentions the event : "About 10 o'clock the Market Place and Streets (of Norwich) were lined with People, and almost all with Wodehouse's cockades in their Hats . . . I got 6 cockades, all for Wodehouse, 3 of them blue and pink, with Wodehouse's name wrote in Silver on the blue, and the others plain blue and pink for my Servants at home. About 11 o'clock, Sir John Wodehouse, preceded with a great many Flaggs and a band of Musick, made his public Entry on horseback, attended with between two and three thousand Men on Horseback." Wodehouse and Astley were elected, but the latter got little applause having voted with Coke against the popular Mr. Pitt.

*   *   *   *   *

But Coke is best remembered for the stimulus he gave to agriculture. In this respect he has become almost a legendary figure and was not in fact the instigator of all the improvements attributed to him. It has been said of the Holkham district "all you will see will be a blade of grass and two rabbits fighting for it", and that the thin sandy soil might be ploughed "by two rabbits yoked to a pocket knife." But his great uncle at Holkham had already drained marshes, planting trees as wind breaks, and to keep off drifting sand, and was growing clover, turnips, lucerne, and wheat. Of the latter it has been stated that none was grown before Billy Coke's time between Holkham and Lynn, and that farming was of the most primitive type. Yet when Arthur Young, the agriculturalist, made his "Farmer's Tour through the East of England", in 1771, before Billy Coke came to Holkham, he noted the good farming and growing of wheat by Mr. Carr of Massingham, and the same at Warham, three miles east of Holkham, where Sir John Turner had introduced a system of crop rotation . . . Nevertheless Coke conferred enormous benefits on Norfolk agriculture, and the rent roll of his Holkham estate rose from £2,000 to £20,000 during his lifetime. He recognised that the interests of landlord and farmer cannot be dissociated, and granted long leases. He introduced South Down sheep into the county, which were in many ways an improvement on the original breed. Unfortunately in so doing the original Norfolk breed was almost extinguished, which was a pity as the sheep had great hardiness, and mutton of a fine flavour.

Coke was a countryman by inclination, and a man of simple tastes. In his early life he had been accustomed to rise before dawn, visit the dairy, and persuade the dairymaid to give him a mug of cream. He then went to the bake-house, pulled the crusty ends from the hot loaves, dipped them in cream, and made a breakfast of them. After that, he would go out on horseback for an excursion. In an age when the labouring man often lived in a leaking straw-thatched hovel, fear of unemployment and the poorhouse ever before him, drunkenness his only escape from misery, Coke's people had serviceable cottages with neat gardens. On his estate there was no poverty as poverty was reckoned in those days; no honest man feared dismissal, for there was always work for more hands. The poorhouse was pulled down because it had no inmates, the two ale-houses closed for lack of customers. For the old people, Coke anticipated the Welfare State by building them dwellings on one floor. The young had instruction in farming matters, much of which he did himself. In the season of flowering grasses, he sent the children to search for seeds of useful varieties. A clever boy had opportunity and encouragement to better himself in Coke's service. William Cobbett, who hated landlords, admitted that Coke's tenants "made use of expressions towards him which affectionate children use towards their parents".

Every summer, for forty years, a gathering took place at Holkham called "Coke's Clippings". To the sheep shearing came farmers, scientists, anyone interested in agriculture, from all parts of the country and beyond the seas, to exchange ideas, and inspect the famous estate. All were entertained in a splendid fashion ; anyone could speak his mind upon agriculture, but discussion of politics was not tolerated. It was at a Clippings that someone made this memorable speech. "Maister Coke and gentlemen, what I wish to say is if more landlords would do as Maister Coke do, they 'ouldnt do as they do do," (which was badly).

Coke represented Norfolk as a Knight of the Shire almost continuously for 43 years. He was a hater of bloodshed, and was accused of being a Bonapartist. This was not correct, but he was opposed to our making the French Revolution a motive for war with France. He retired from politics in 1832, a significant year to mark the exit of a great Whig, for the Reform Bill set the seal on much that he had laboured for. Though he had been offered a peerage seven times, it was not till 1837 that Coke accepted an earldom, choosing the title of Earl of Leicester and Holkham. He was the first peer created by the young Queen.

Coke was twice married; by his first wife, who died in 1800, he had three daughters. His second wife, Lady Ann Keppel, was his godchild, and only 18 at the time of her marriage in 1822; she had four sons and a daughter.

Coke died in 1842, aged 88. A great monument was erected to his memory in Holkham Park, but he is more sweetly remembered by other stones in little bridges, spanning lonely streams. The water gurgles through pasture, and tall grasses caress the deep-cut initials—T.W.C.

JAMES POINTER

JAMES POINTER was born in 1868, in a solitary cottage called "Peewit", below the slope of the fields. He was a small wiry boy, and his first job was that of garden boy at the Hall. By this time his parents had moved to a house near the Mill, in the neighbouring Market Town. James walked across the meadows to the Hall. which was a "gothic style" house nearly surrounded by trees. The site of the Old Hall was near the lake, below the house, but there was nothing left of it except ruined walls. There were three gardeners at the Hall, and only one boy, for Bigoty, the head man, used to say "two boys are half a boy." Early in life, James took to keeping pet birds. He had sampled young magpies, but they "weren't muchers." At this time he had a jackdaw, which went to work with him, and he shut it in a disused stokehole. Unhappily, one day, Jack got out, and lighted on the Mistress's straw hat, which was decorated with imitation fruit. She screamed, Bigoty appeared, and the matter leaked out, so that was the end of the bird's coming to the Hall. One day Jack disappeared. Heartbroken, James searched for him, and at length he spied Jack in a cage, in the window of a cottage kept by an old man. James asked for his bird, but the man was abusive, and would not take the half-crown which James offered him, and was all he had.

After a few years, James Pointer left to better himself and went to the garden of an old gentleman in the Town. Here he was second man to Sapy. His master took in half an acre of meadow for extra kitchen garden, and James helped to lay the brick edging by the paths. At the age of 28 he began the central and most important stage of his career. He got a job at Bayfield Hall, where there were five gardeners. James was now married, and was given a cottage at Glandford. In November 1897, the sea surged up the Glaven valley to his very threshold. "I aint a-going to stop in that there willage and get drownded", he told his master, so he was moved into half of a double flint and brick house on the opposite side of the road to the Hall drive.

As years went on, a friendship matured between master and man. James was quick-witted, but slow of speech, and he always had an apt answer for the little baronet. Besides hoeing gravel paths (which he did to perfection), clipping edges, and "tricolating up" flower beds, he sometimes did jobs in the Hall, and scrubbed floor bricks with milk and water. Outside, peafowl were his bane, nipping off flower heads and "one o' them ol' peacocks saw hisself in the winders, and jabbed inter 'em and broke 'em". One day he was told to take a live peacock to a neighbour as a present, "so I dropped on ter that ol' bird, and put him in a sack".

James was athletic, and his master no sportsman, so when the Harriers met at Bayfield he was bidden to mount a horse and go with them. "The moment that there hoss heard the bougal, that went off like tally-ho." His master was a widower and childless. James accompanied him into the West Country to stay with his sister. They passed through London and put up at an hotel, "where they gave you so many prongs you don't know what ter do with 'em". And there was not enough food to satisfy James's appetite, "so I had to go round the corner ter git some more". James went to Kew, and took in all its wonders, and to "that there market garden at Wisley". Arriving at their destination, James was sent to a cinema with the Cook—a new experience. He sat straight up on the flap of his chair, not knowing the seat would turn down. "How much longer du this here last?", he enquired after a few minutes.

* * * * *

In the 1914-18 war James Pointer was too old for the Services, and became a Special Constable ; and he served again in this respect during the 1939-45 conflict. Not that he was ever a Constable in the modern acceptance of the word ; he just walked by night to find out what was moving. He said "this here war ain't narthin' like the last with them there Zeppelins buzzing about. Now that's the aeroplanes what come and settle above you." The dull thud of distant bombs broke the night. "Hallo! Hallo! so there he go, and I reckon he's mistook this time 'cause there's narthin' only mash where he's a-droppin' them." After that he went to bed and to sleep until morning, for "What will come, will come". Early in the war, James did not fear the German aeroplanes by day. "If he see me in the garden he 'ont waste no bombs on me." But later he changed his mind "acause them there Garmans have got reg-lar crafty, they come flightin' out o' the clouds with there little ol' guns, so I took and dodged into the alder carr".

In 1929 it was obvious that the baronet's life was drawing to a close. The doctor sent a nurse, but he was angry. "Can't I give orders in my own house?" he said, "send her up to Holt station in the pony cart". He told James to look after him. "I'm a rum sort of butler, I am", said the gardener. "You'll do" was the reply. So he sat in the old man's room, and the quiet hours slipped by in the darkened house. At length the end came ; the last baronet of his line was carried by his men from Glandford church, where they had laid him, past the Hall and through the Park to Letheringsett. A hundred of his people followed him, and the walk took one and a half hours. His only memorial was a small lozenge-shaped stone, bearing the initials A.J. "All he told me he wanted was dawg's stun" said James. Although the gardener had been left a small farmhouse in a neighbouring village, he put his daughter into it, and chose to stay where he was ; nobody had the heart to turn him out.

After that he sought other employment, and went to the garden in the Market Town of the old gentleman he had served in the 1890s. The daughter-in-law took him for several days a week, and here he worked for many more years, in his steady methodical way. He went also to a small garden where the lawn "weren't no bigger than what two pigeons could play on". Eventually his mistress died, and her daughter took over. One morning James brought bad news—his wife had died suddenly. The local welfare officer found him a housekeeper, and brought her up to the garden for James' inspection. But he was busy, and would not stop to interview her. "She'll do", he said. But she did not do, being old and infirm, and a short time afterwards she had a stroke. James ministered to her all night, still wearing his slush boots, but she had to be taken to hospital. Another housekeeper was found, who served him well.

By now James Pointer was getting a very old man, but his energy and interest never seemed to flag. All day long he would go on digging, with the "collier" dog sitting beside him, sometimes on newly-sown ground. "That dawg, he don't do no harm", he said. Now and then he took the solace of his pipe, but he always put it away hastily when anybody approached. He had a great love of flowers, even wild ones in the wrong place. "That there convolvulus, that's a pretty thing, I 'ont touch it." But ground elder, "ol' Hilder", was his special enemy. The summer of 1959 was hot. James hoed a path in the full glare of the after-noon sun. Urged to find a cooler spot, he retorted "I can't stop work, not for the sun". At 6 p.m. he would be at work still—nobody could make him leave off.

95

Winter came, and in the New Year James reset the brick edging which he had helped to lay nearly 70 years before. One day, on returning home, he noticed a heap of gravel-sand on top of the little hill near his house, which would do for a path, so he went to fetch a barrow load. The neighbour came out, and wanted to "crowd" the barrow for him, but the old man would not give up. That night he had a heart attack and lay-abed. He had a cold little room, the window looking north. "If they don't let me out, I shall be a-flying out o' the winder", he said, "them birds will be gettin' the peas". A few days later he died, and was buried in Glandford churchyard. He was 92, and with him a presence had gone from the neighbourhood. Unconsciously a poet in his speech, witty, with a zest for life, and a love of children and animals, his like would be hard to find to-day.

PEOPLE AT LYNN
(The Burneys)

UPON a day in the 1750s, Charles Burney rode away on his mare, Peggy. He went by the rising road to the north-east, till the Fen country spanned out behind him. Ahead, the heathy uplands tumbled into blue distance, but Charles Burney had no eye for natural beauties. Letting his reins hang loose, he pulled from his pocket a book of Italian poetry, which he began to translate with the aid of a dictionary. Anon, he stuffed his book away, for his friend's words kept coming into his mind. "Is not settling at Lynn planting your youth, genius, hopes, etc. against a north wall? Can you expect high flavoured fruit from such an aspect?"

Burney, the organist, did not expect it. The organ, he admitted, was "execrably bad", the "foggy alderman" totally indifferent to music, and "the local Apollo", Sir John Turner, "extremely shallow". Charles Burney was going to Holkham, and afterwards, perhaps, to visit Sir John at Warham. He found the society of country houses preferable to that of Lynn, where there was more high living than high thinking, and he liked Sir John well enough in his remote retreat.

But these roads, how bad they were! Afterwards, when travelling abroad, Burney described the road between Potsdam and Berlin as "through a deep running sand, like the worst parts of Norfolk and Suffolk".

It was ill-health that drove Burney to a ten-year sojourn at Lynn. The trade of that ancient port was then considerable, though silting had led to a decline in prosperity. The draining of the Fens had given the town access, by the river Ouse, to farm products ; coal, Port wine from Spain, came to Lynn for home consumption ; ships sailed out to Greenland and Spitzbergen for whale ; others returned with spices from the West Indies and the Spanish Main. These last vessels were armed, sometimes merely "for adventure"—a polite name for raids on far imperial Spain.

At Lynn, masts towered above the roof tops ; warehouses were crammed with merchandise, with corn and beer for export. In the dark odorous alleys and on the teeming

97

quays, strange tongues mingled with Norfolk voices. In fine houses lived the families of merchant princes, who ruled the social and commercial life of the town. In 1760, Burney returned to London, where his career began to blossom gloriously. But his life was saddened by the loss of his wife, and in 1767 he married again, Mrs. Stephen Allen, widow of a Lynn merchant. His first wife on her death-bed, had advised him to marry the intelligent but plain Miss Young, of the town, but, as his daughter remarked afterwards, "He was too ardent an admirer of beauty to dispense in totality with that attractive embellishment of the female form". Charles—Doctor Burney as he was soon to become—had a long life, dying as the short peace was celebrated the year before Waterloo. As a musician, he was a brilliant performer ; he composed music, and wrote an exhaustive study of its history, for which he toured the Continent. Poor Charles, how he suffered from sea-sickness when crossing the Channel ! Wearied from the malady, he fell asleep in his bunk upon reaching Dover harbour, and awoke to find himself halfway to Calais again!

Burney was a very agreeable character ; he had no enemies and many friends, among them the great men of the day. "I love Dr. Burney", declared Dr. Johnson, "my heart goes out to meet him. Dr. Burney is a man for all the world to love. It is but natural to love him."

When Burney had been in Lynn about a year and a half, his second daughter, Fanny was born, but the child only emerges upon the screen of history sixteen years later. By then the family had moved to London, but spent summer holidays in the Norfolk town, occupying a house belonging to the second Mrs. Burney. In the little parlour, which her father used as a dressing-room, the small dark-skinned girl, with the sharp nose and mouse-coloured hair, began the diary, which was to be a beam of light on the world of her day. Fanny had been a backward girl, not being able to read till the age of eight, but at sixteen she could not help scribbling. Her step-mother did not approve of it. Nothing could be less desirable or elegant than that a young lady should write, but write she did—for the next sixty years—till her failing eye-sight checked her busy quill. Oh that her scrupulousness had not made her burn or erase all that she considered might be mischievous ! Fanny had little affection for Lynn. "Such a set of tittle, tattle, prittle, prattle visitants ! Oh dear ! I am sick of the ceremony and fuss of these fall-lall people. So much chitchat, complimentary nonsense—in short a country town is my detestation. All the conversation is scandal, all the attention, dress, and almost all the heart folly, envy, and censoriousness . . . we live here, generally speaking, in a very regular way. We breakfast always at 10, and rise as much before as we please—we dine precisely at 2, drink tea about 6 and sup exactly at 9. I make a rule never to indulge myself in my two most favourite pursuits, reading and writing, in the morning.

But, in the afternoon, she went to the "Cabin", the "pleasantest place belonging to this house". It is sometimes called the Look-out, as ships are observed from here. Fanny's step-sister, Maria Allen, writing some years after from her new house in Lynn said, "We have a very large look-out, which overlooks the river. We never have any ships lying against our watergate, at least very seldom to what we had there (at the Burneys) by which means we escape the oaths and ribaldry of the sailors and porters, which used to drive us from thence." Fanny may never have visited Lynn after her early twenties, but who can escape the influence of early environment? In her dreams and in her mind's eye, Fanny must have carried the Norfolk scene through her long eventful life.

Fanny's first and best novel, *Evelina*, was published anonymously when she was twenty-five. But the secret soon leaked out. "Next to the balloon, Miss Burney is the object of private curiosity", wrote Mrs. Barbauld, another novelist. Till her thirty-fifth year, Fanny lived in the world of wit and fashion. She knew Burke, Wyndham, Johnson, Garrick, Sheridan, and Mrs. Thrale. Then, in 1786, a strange fate overtook her—she was appointed Dresser to the Queen. Letters of congratulation came from her friends, but poor Fanny, who seldom cried, blotted her manuscript with tears. She entered the Court as a regretful nun to a convent. The atmosphere was austere, the conversation of equerries and ladies in waiting hardly as scintillating as that to which Fanny had been accustomed. Unsuited to her duties, she nevertheless bore them patiently for five years. There fell to her, however, one task to which she was eminently suitable—the attendance at the trial of Warren Hastings, which she reported for the Queen. At last, ill health afforded her an excuse to escape from her position, and she was released with a pension of £100 a year. "It is but her due, she has given five years of her pen", said George III.

*   *   *   *   *

A few years later, Fanny married General D'Arblay, a French *émigre*, and it was a love match. At the beginning of the new century, Fanny and her husband went to France,

99

where she was detained for ten years owing to the resumption of war. Fanny outlived her generation and her talent. A forlorn shade of the eighteenth century, she lingered on to Queen Victoria's reign.

Dr. Burney was the father of six children by his first wife. His eldest son, James, entered the Navy whilst the family was at Lynn. He sailed with Captain Cooke, and, like his sister, had literary ability. Charles, the younger son, was also born at Lynn, and became one of the first classical scholars in Europe. But he seems to have been a dull fellow compared with his sailor brother. Southey wrote of how he met Charles Burney (the younger), "who after a long silence broke out into a discourse upon the properties of the conjunction, quam . . . it was a relief to leave him, and find his brother, the Captain, smoking after supper, and letting out puffs at one corner of his mouth, and puns at the other." James was nicknamed "The Admiral", and, as an old man, longed for the rank in earnest. Through the efforts of his friends, his wish was granted ; a few weeks before his death he became Rear-Admiral James Burney.

PHILLIP SKIPPON'S JOURNEYS

EVEN 300 years ago people were extremely interested in the weather as they are now, and it was just as wayward then. Phillip Skippon, described as "a scientific man and a traveller", wrote in 1672, "some countrymen observe it usually proves a wet summer if crows and magpies, etc., build their nests on ye highest branches of trees ; and when they build on the lower branches it will prove dry". Phillip had milder occupations than his father, who was one of Cromwell's Major-Generals, in fact, he was one of the two most notable Norfolk soldiers of the Civil War, the other being Sir Jacob Astley, who fought for the King. Major-General Skippon was severly wounded in the head at Naseby, was in charge of the guard during a period of King Charles's captivity, but refused to serve as one of the commissioners at his trial. He was said to have "gotten a vast estate", which included the Bishop's Palace at Norwich. His family came from Weasenham, and he also inherited property at Foulsham.

Phillip, the younger, inherited the "Capital messuage and mansion at Foulsham, with his dove, malt, mill, and brew houses," but he lived at Wrentham in Suffolk, and only visited Foulsham from time to time. In 1668, he took a journey from London into Norfolk, which he entered through Brandon. He wrote "Ye cheese made in Norff is generally of a whiter colour than I have observed elsewhere" (it had a reputation of being inferior). The harvest men "beg largesse of passengers etc., when they receive any they hallow (shout) several times." He also remarked that "the honey nigh ye coasts of Norff is better than within the country, because there is no heath flower nor buck wheat neare ye shore". And he wrote down a Norfolk proverb. "He that plants willow shall buy a horse before he that plants oaks shall buy a saddle."

One of Phillip Skippon's journeys took him from Foulsham to Yarmouth, through Horningtoft, Brisley, Billingford, Lenwade, Attlebridge, Felthorpe, Stratton Strawless, Caulshill (this old spelling is the right way to pronounce "Coltishall") and Ludham. "I observed about 4 miles before I came to Yarmouth a westerly wind blowing hard, ye waters in one of ye marshes looked very greene and

101

stunk, ye waves beating on ye shore made a greate froth."

He found the Yarmouth herring fishery very considerable. "In a covered room they make many smothering fires of wood under ye herrings, as they hang from ye very top till the reach of a man." He saw also salt-pans "nigh this towne", and noted the narrow coaches with solid wooden wheels, which could pass along the rows. Yarmouth people had a disappointment in 1681 for "Ye Towne-Hall was newly beautyfied, and other preparations making, but his Majesty came not". (Charles II.) After leaving Yarmouth, Skippon "rode by ye sea on ye sand, and came through Caisters". He passed over Bastwick bridge and Ludham, and went northward, "having past in sight of Wursted on my left hand, thence I went thorow N.Walsham, a pretty market towne, ye houses mostly pan tiled and built of stone. Ye market place is upon ye descent of a hill . . . Ye villages lye very close in most partes of Norffolke, but here thicker than elsewhere, w'ch occasions this Rhyme :

Gimingham, Trimingham, Knapton & Trunch,
North Repps and S. Repps are all of a bunch.

The Towne of Cromer was formerly considerable for fishing, but is now very poore. The Sea hath washed in a great many houses & every yeare it eats away part of ye cliffe, when there are spring tides or much frosty weather . . . Cambridge and Newmarket is served with fish from hence. About 20 little fisherboats belong to Cromer".

He went on through Runton, Beeston, and Sheringham to Weybourne, "about ¼ mi. from ye village I rode to ye Beach of stones wch begins hereabouts & runs for 3 miles towds Cley, ye shore is levell with ye sea in this place, & this great beach of small stones keeps off ye violence of ye sea, there are two banks in this beach, ye nearest ye sea is ye lowest . . . From Weybourne after I ascended a steepe hill, I travelled 3 miles over a large heath, covered with ling, & past thorow Holt, a market towne." After that, he went through Edgefield, Wood Dalling and Salle to Attlebridge, where he lodged the night. The next night he stayed at Diss, and went on to Bungay and Beccles. "Yarmouth is served with much beere from this place, ye water of ye towne being somewhat brackish There is a convenient passage by water from Beckles to Yarmouth almost every day or night, every passenger paying 4d. a piece ; ye like conveniently from Yarm: to Norwich for sixpence a piece."

Phillip Skippon noticed that many of the churches were thatched, and most of the houses, and was told good thatch lasted from seven to ten years. "Spinning of wooll with a rock & spindle & knitting of stocking employes great numbers of poore in most of ye county. The women walk up & downe as they spin & knitt, they can knitt a stockin in a day." About sixty years after this, Daniel Defoe, who made a Norfolk journey, remarked that "Aylsham is a poor town noted for knitters, Fakenham noted for nothing but for having salt-pits formerly". Defoe approved of the country between Cromer and Norwich, and said it was "exceedingly fertile as well in corn as pasture. The pheasants (which are very pleasant to behold) were in such great plenty as to be seen in the stubble like cocks and hens ; a testamony (by the way) that the country has more tradesmen than gentlemen in it."

Skippon, on another journey from Thetford to Northwold and Methwold, remarked that the latter was "a very poore market towne. The country hereabouts is champion ground bearing good corne. Within 3 miles of Northold (Northwold) is Stoke, on a river that carryes boats to Lyn and other parts. Very good pasture and meadow ground in Northold, and fenny commons where they feed great heards of Cattle".

The winter of 1669 was very cold. "Variety of water foule in ye marshes and broadwater neare the sea. The liquor in my Roman glasse at ye coldest, sunke to 11 and 12." And he describes a very severe winter in 1673, when in March "This cold snowy season ye crowes and magpies pick'd the flesh off living cowes backs."

Phillip Skippon was knighted at Whitehall in 1674 and died in 1692.

THE MERE UNCOUNTED FOLK

How did Norfolk people fare in days gone by, "the mere uncounted folk"? Contemporary records of one sort and another, and diaries throw light on the lives of the well-to-do. There are few annals of the poor, but there are some. In many a Norfolk church chest lie bundles of discoloured papers which reveal fragments of the stories of those who became down and out, for they were important to parishes because of the law of settlement.

The break up of private armies after the Wars of the Roses, the decay of the feudal system, the conversion of arable land into sheep-walk, and later the dissolution of the monasteries, all contributed to the number of vagrants and beggars who roamed the country in Tudor times. An attempt was made to maintain the destitute out of charitable funds ; bishops were to assist by gentle exhortations, but the voluntary method failed, and legislation culminated in the Poor Law Act of 1603-4. Under it churchwardens, and four, three, or two, substantial householders of the parish were nominated yearly as Overseers of the Poor, with the duties of setting the jobless to work, and relieving the maimed, aged, and infirm, money being raised for this by a compulsory parish rate. Incorrigible vagabonds could be transported to the plantations. The qualifications of a genuine parishioner were later defined by Settlement Laws. Settlement could be gained by birth, if parents were legally settled in a parish, by bastardy, if the mother " 'belonged' to the parish, by renting a tenement of the value of £10, serving a parochial office, or an apprenticeship, or fulfilling a contract as a yearly servant". A destitute person who was deemed not to belong to a parish, after telling his or her life-story before a magistrate, was removed to the place of last legal settlement. This might entail a journey of a hundred miles or so, escort being provided by the parish constables en route. Life-stories of the unfortunate, told before one or more magistrates, were carefully copied down, and kept for possible future reference, and these documents were known as Examinations of Paupers as to Settlement.

When John Catton was examined in Holt on July 12th, 1806, he was "a private soldier in his Majesty's Troop of

Artillery now stationed at Colchester", and, apparently, his wife, and baby daughter, Mary Ann, were then living at Holt without the means of support. John said that "to the best of his knowledge and belief he was born in Wedlock in the parish of Great Massingham in the County of Norfolk, and that he is about twenty-five years of age. When he was about sixteen years of age he Let himself on old Michaelmas Day to William Yearham (his Grandfather) at East Beckham, as Second Man, and received a Shilling for hire, and for his Year's Service, he was to receive his Board and Lodging, and his Master to find him Cloathes in lieu of Wages". John worked for his grandfather for a year and a half, but seems not to have been satisfied with his employment for "he Bound himself Apprentice by Indenture to Mr. Hurry, a Merchant Ship Owner of Great Yarmouth, to serve him as a Mariner on board some or one of his ships Haling from the Port of Yarmouth. That he duly entered upon his Apprenticeship, and served on board one of such Ships about 5 Weeks, during which Time she made one Voyage to Russia, and on her return to London this Examinant was Impressed and put on Board his Majesty's Ship *Sandwich* at the Noar and afterwards on Board the *Prince*, Capt. Larkham, and served in that Ship more than Seven Years, and was then Discharged at Plymouth, at the conclusion of the last War . . . he returned to Norfolk and "went and Wrought as a Weekly Man with Wm. Yearham his Uncle (who succeeded his Grandfather in the Farm at East Beckham)". Here John Catton stayed for about a year, during which time he married in Holt, but his wife, Mary, belonged to Hindolveston. At the midsummer, John, who was restless once more ,"Inlisted himself into the Corps wherein he now serves", leaving his wife and child lodging with Mr. Platten in Holt. John was no scholar, and he signed his statement with a cross. Here we lose sight of him, but there is record of the warships he served aboard . . . H.M.S. *Sandwich* was an old second-rate vessel, fitted out as a Receiving Ship after much service.

H.M.S. *Prince* was also second-rate but not so old as the *Sandwich*. She was one of the ships blockading Brest, and was present at Trafalgar, but John Catton was not aboard her then. When he joined the Navy, willy-nilly, there was still no uniform for Ratings. A customary dress was coming into fashion, though a decent suit of clothes would pass muster with captains. Pigtails were worn, petticoats, white trousers, blue jackets, and tarpaulin hats were becoming usual, as were straw hats.

John Jeary knew the call of the sea too. When he was about 12 years old he went with his uncle "on board of a sloop called the *Sea Nymph* which was chiefly in the Coal trade, and sailed from Cley in Norfolk, but after two or three years my father persuaded me to go to some trade, as he did not like me to continue at Sea. I then, with the assent of my father, was bound apprentice to Mr. Chapling, a Shoemaker at Holt for four years, by an indenture . . . regularly signed." Jeary almost completed his term, "but not liking the business, with the assent of my master, Chapling, I left him and I went to Sea again. The first ship I went in was a vessel belonging to Mr. Mann of Cley". After some years as a sailor, John Jeary had another go at shoemaking, "I was occasionally at Sea and occupied as a Shoemaker till about thirty years ago, when I was placed in the Customs at Clay as a tide Waiter and Boatman, which situation I now hold . . . My father's Settlement was, I believe at Clay, he at the time of his death possessing a house in that place. Witness my hand this 11th day of September 1824."

Some men joined the Army, and William Stephenson confessed at Ely in 1819 that he was very young at the time. Born at Holt in Norfolk, he lived with his family there till "he was about seven years of age—that then he entered into the West Norfolk Regiment of Militia, his Father being in the same at that time, in which he continued for about twenty-six years and a half when he was discharged. That when he had been in the said Regiment of Militia for about thirteen years he was married to Sarah his present wife, by whom he hath not any Children". William had not left the Army more than nine months when he was balloted into the Cambridgeshire Militia, in which he had to serve over five years. The Militia, "the Constitutional Force" was recruited by volunteers and by ballot. Balloted men had to serve or find substitutes. After he left the Force, Stephenson "wrought as a Cordwainer" (shoemaker). He had heard his brother say that their father's legal settlement was at Holt, which he gained by serving an apprenticeship there.

The Army had an attraction for Walter Fowle, who was 70 years of age when he was examined at Holt in 1811. He had never known his father, who had died when he was an infant, and his mother remarried to "one Nathaniel Fox of Holt, Butcher." When Walter was 10 or 11 he "went and wrought with his Brother as a Bricklayers Labourer at Creak for three-Quarters of a Year . . . that he then returned to his Mother at Holt, and when he was about 14 Years old he went upon liking to one Bond, a Baker of Wells, to whom he was to have been Bound Apprentice". But this did not suit him for after nine months "he inlisted himself as a private in his late Majesty's 71st Regiment of Foot, and served therein about 4 Years and a half, when the Regiment was broke, and he was discharged and returned Home to Holt. And then Clubbed himself for a Year to one John Franks a Baker, to be instructed in the business." Walter was content to spend just over a year with the baker "and then left him, and rambled the Country without any fixed place of Residence for better than 12 Months, and then inlisted into his present Majesty's Royal Artillery. He served for more than seven years in this corps, returned home for a short space, and then again inlisted into the same Service, and Served therein until the 30th Day of June 1807, when he was Discharged from further Service with a Pension or Allowance of 1/10½ per Diem." During his travels, Walter had married at Edinburgh, and had children, three of whom survived and were all married and provided for. Like many others, Walter Fowle could only sign his mark.

Many young people were educated for their trade by serving an apprenticeship for periods of between three and seven years. Indentures were signed, and premiums paid either by the apprentice's family, or, in the case of the poorer sort, by the Parish. The latter were called Town Boys, and crafty overseers would arrange for the apprenticeships to be served without the parish, apprenticeship carrying a settlement. But often an apprenticeship was broken, generally by mutual consent. Henry Nobes of Briston was apprenticed at 14 to James Clarke of Holt, glover, for the term of 7 years. He was "boarded and lodged with his Master, who found him all necessaries".

The glover had been paid a premium of £30 by Brinton, for though Henry Nobes lived at Briston, his father had a settlement in the former parish. This apprenticeship lasted for 6 years, till Henry was 20, "when having had a dispute with his Master, he ran away, and never afterwards returned to his service." He went to Newton Flotman, and then to London, where he got employment, and married in the church of St. Pancras. Apparently, after about a year, Henry Nobes began to yearn for home, for he "came down to Briston to see his Friends, when he was apprehended by his Master, James Clarke, for leaving his service before the expiration of his apprenticeship. That (he) agreed with his Master to give him 4£ for leaving his service, 2£ of which sum he paid him down, and the remainder he was to pay as soon as he could." Henry Nobes does not seem to have been a law-abiding subject, for "soon afterwards was apprehended upon a charge of felony, and transported, and returned to this country last September" (1827).

Henry Nobes must have been away for about 6 years, for he was 27 when his examination was taken. Now, he and his wife (there was one child) had become chargeable to the parish of Holt.

It was not always the fault of the apprentice that an apprenticeship was broken. When James Pearson was 16 he left his home at North Barningham in the year 1810, and was "Bound Apprentice by a regular Indenture (of which there was only one part which was held by his Master) to Robert Sunman of Gresham, Cordwainer, for the Term of Four Years, on the following Terms. His Master to find him lodging in his House the whole time and Constant Employment, and to Teach him the Trade, for which he was to take the whole of his Earnings the first Year, and one half of the same the remaining three Years, and the Examinant to have the remaining half, and to Board and Clothe himself". After a year or so, Sunman went to live in Sheringham, taking his apprentice with him, but here they quarrelled, in consequence of his Master's neglecting to find him Employment in the Trade, insomuch as they went before John Gay Esq. a Magistrate . . . who after hearing both parties directed the Examinant's Father (who was there present) if the Master did not in future find him employment and Teach him . . . to take (him) away, and let him get work elsewhere". James had another attempt to get on with his master, "where he staid a few Days, but his Master still neglecting him as before, the Examinant left him, but his Master still held the Indenture . . . and about a Year ago he applied to his Master, Sunman . . . who said he had Searched for it but could not find the same, and that it might have been lost or destroyed for ought he knew to the contrary". When he left the unsatisfactory Sunman, James went to work as a "journey-man" (one employed by the day) to a shoemaker in Gresham for nearly a year, and then to James Frankland of Holt, another cordwainer. "After Working for him for a Week, he paid him what his work came to by the price, and then told him he was not forward enough in the Business, and therefore would not suit him, unless he underwent some further Instructions". Therefore, it was verbally agreed that James Pearson should "Work for the said James Frankland for 12 Months, and be Instructed in the Business, and paid 2/6 per Week Wages, and he to find himself in Board and lodging, but nevertheless he was to go and make his Harvest in that Year, and whatever Time he was Absent at Harvest he was to make good to his Master when Harvest was ended". James stayed with Frankland for two years, being away at harvest for five weeks on each occasion. Whilst he was at Sheringham with his former master, James Pearson had been "duly Appointed to the Office of Clerk (for North Barningham) at an annual Salary of £1.5 and the Privileges of all Fees for Marriages and Funerals, and has continued to Execute that Office for and on his own Account". Although of very slender means he had married, and had three children under four. After leaving his last master, he does not seem to have worked, except, presumably, at odd jobs. Perhaps the family was in need of relief, or the Holt overseer suspected that it would require help from the parish. This was a tricky case of settlement, and the Magistrates were unable to decide to which parish James Pearson belonged. Counsel's opinion had to be sought, and it was decided that he had a settlement at Sheringham, because of his service there as an apprentice some years before.

Some people were very young when they went to work. Joseph Butters was five when he "went to live with Mr. Banks of Holt, surgeon, as stable boy". Marriage was often at an early age. John Ramm, a farmer's boy, was under sixteen when "with his Father's consent was lawfully Married by Licence in the parish Church of Cromer." Some fell sick ; Thomas Pells was living at Holt with his family when "he went home to Briston with the Ague, and was Maintained in the Workhouse there several Weeks". Ague was what we call now Malaria, and was common in Norfolk. A tradition says it died out in the last two decades of the 18th century, but must have lingered on after that. In 1780 it was said of a stranger on his "first coming into the county, that he is arrested by the Bailiff of Marshland". Parson Woodforde's servant suffered from ague. "My Man Briton whilst he was waiting at dinner, was taken in the Ague, and he went directly and plunged himself Head and Ears in my great Pond in the Garden, after which I gave him a good dram of Gin and put him to bed, where he laid and slept about 3 Hours. He then got up and was brave after."

Service for a year as a yearly servant gave a settlement, and some masters were crafty enough to make a contract of only 51 weeks, and pay the man separately for the final one. William Chapman of Edgefield was treated thus by William Stannard, a Holt farmer. Stannard engaged Chapman for 51 weeks, and at the expiration thereof the latter asked his master for his wages, and was told "he had no time then, and to go on with his work, and the Examin-and continued to do so till the Michaelmas day, when his Master paid him his wages for 51 weeks (£4.10 but he boarded and lodged in the farmhouse) and 1/6 for his week's service over the 51 weeks, and then hired him again for 51 weeks more".

John Moy was 24 when he was examined in 1800. He had been born at Foulsham where his parents lived under a certificate, for their settlement was in Guestwick. When John was 13 or 14 "he Let himself for a Year to John Thompson, of Foulsham, Surgeon, which Service he duly performed . . . That some short time after Christmas in the Year 1796 he was informed by his Mother of one, John Wood, who had lived some time in the Service of The Rev. Mr. Johnson then of Holt, that his Son was now dead, and consequently Mr. Johnson wanted a Servant". So John Moy went to see Mr. Johnson and was told by him that "he did not hire any", but that "if he liked to come and live with him until he could better himself he might, this Examinant asked him what he would give him from that time to Michaelmas, Mr. Johnson replied I shall not hire you nor make any Agreement about Wages." The result was John Moy went to serve Mr. Johnson, and stayed till the following Old Michaelmas day without any Contract, but his Master gave him at different times three or four Shillings as Pocket Money, and upon the Old Michaelmas day . . . not having suited himself with another place, his Master told him he might go on as usual . . . to which he replied very well, and continued . . . until about Ten Weeks of the following Michaelmas, when he and his Master being in Norwich (he) was informed that Barnwell Esq. of East Dereham wanted a Servant. John told his master this who replied "Very well John, if you think this place will Suit you and you can get it, do so you may go and welcome".

Whereupon John Moy went to see Mr. Barnwell who then enquired of Mr. Johnson of his "Character and qualifications, and then hired him to go into the Service within a fortnight, and to stay till the following Michaelmas". When John left his old master's house he was given "a Guinea and a half for the Time he had been there, and so they parted". He served Mr. Barnwell for a full year, and after that must have had only casual employment, but he was married at Wood Norton in 1800, and must have gone to live at Hindolveston, for he and his wife had become chargeable to that parish.

A girl could be apprenticed in the same manner as a lad, for instance in housewifery, but there is no case in the Holt examinations of this procedure, though parish officers sometimes put out Town Girls to serve as domestic servants. Martha Everett had an unfortunate experience before she was twenty-six. She was born in Holt about 1800, and apparently lived with her parents there till she was sixteen when she went to serve Mr. Baker at Runton for the best part of a year, and then returned to her parents who were living in Holt workhouse. Later her father received a letter from another daughter, who was living at Woolwich, asking if Martha could go and nurse her during the time of her lying-in. So Martha went to Woolwich in the November, and looked after her sister till the following March. Then she went to work at the Sign of *Sir John Falstaff* in Southwark, for the wages of 2/3 per week, where she stayed for eighteen months. Afterwards, "being pregnant by Thomas Payne, the Son of Thomas Payne (her master) she was unable to go through her daily work, but continued living in Thomas Payne's house for four Months, when her Mistress, about a Month before her confinement provided her with a lodging at a Mr. Arnolds in some other part of London totally unknown to this Examinant . . . to which she was taken in a Hacking Coach, between nine and ten o'clock at Night, and to which Lodging her Mistress, Mrs. Payne, accompanied her, and then left her the next day, about twelve o'clock at Noon, when a woman of the name of Gamble came by her Mistress' order to nurse and attend upon her during her confinement." Here she remained for about a month, but what happened to her child is not stated. Anyhow, she was "fetched away by Mrs. Payne about eight o'clock in the evening in a Coach, and returned to her Master's at the *Sir John Falstaff*. That this Examinant continued after her return back with the said Mr. and Mrs. Payne till they quitted the Public house . . . then went with them and resided for about two Years in a House at Kiddle Place, Battle Bridge, opposite the smallpox hospital . . . and was supported by her own Labour and an allowance of five shillings a week from Simon Payne, she occasionally doing Mrs. Payne's work, and working by day at other places."

*   *   *   *   *

Sometimes overseers received heartrending letters, but we wonder if it did rend their hearts? Here is one from Norwich, dated September 30th, 1829. Apparently Hannah Edwards thought she had a settlement in Holt, for she wrote thus to the overseer:
"Sir,
I am sorry to inform you that my Husband Thomas Edwards have Left me and two Children, he Left me intent to go and sike after work, and when he gott to London he heard of a Ship going to America at New York, and he sent me word he was going to America in that Ship. Now, Sir, I and my two Children are Left to God and the wide

World, for, Sir, he toke all the money that he could gitt a Long with him, he Never Left me one Shilling. Now, Sir, I and my Children are Left to your Mercy, and, Sir, if you do not send me Some Relief Next Week I must apply to the Corporation of Norwich . . . and, Sir, I am Sorry to inform you that I am in the Family way, and expect to be Confined some time the Next Month. So, Sir, you must think that I am Left very uncomfortable. But I hope, Sir, that you will be A Friend to me and my Children."

In the end, Hannah and her children entered the Holt workhouse.

These old workhouses were mostly loathsome and squalid, the amount of food and comfort depending upon the generosity of parish officials. But families lived together and in some workhouses perhaps, the inmates existed in more or less happy squalor. The Union workhouses, which replaced them after the harsh New Poor Law Act of 1834 were, probably, even more unpopular. For the Act decreed the separation of families, and that the standard of food should be kept below that outside. It was the fear of these prison-like houses, often built in selected bleak and isolated situations, which haunted the minds of the poor even to the present century.

"Times were hard, them times", but still old England was a comparatively humane and free country. In the pitiful, cold winter, life in sickness and adversity must have been terrible, but in the luxury of summer even the pauper would have found delight as he "rambled the country up and down".

NORFOLK OFFICIALS
OF THE PAST

TO-DAY the election of a churchwarden is unlikely to cause a flutter in the parish, but it was not always so. About the middle of the last century feeling ran high, and a broadsheet was circulated in Holt urging rate-payers not to re-elect one, Mr. Boyd. "His actions have proved that he has thought more of the will of the rich than the wants of the poor." As a trustee of the Lows Common "he would have sent a poor fellow to jail for getting a rabbit to make a dinner for himself and his children . . . and has allowed a very severe winter to pass without any distribution of Coals for the Poor." Mr. Boyd got in nevertheless ; the two churchwardens were principal officers of the Vestry Meeting, which governed the town. But now they can do little more in a civil sense than tell a man to take off his hat in church, or turn out a misbehaver.

The Vestry's mantle has fallen upon the Parish Council, or rather some shred of it. For the Council cannot do very much more than wrangle about the cemetery, the public water closets, the street lights, and levy a small rate. In Holt, there are Vestry minutes for 60 years of the last century, and they give a picture of the development of a small community. Any rate-payer could attend the Vestry Meetings, but in practise only a dozen or so of the well-to-do seem to have been there. The minutes reveal comparatively few entries on ecclesiastical matters, but the abolition of the church rate in 1868 caused Vestrymen to consider ways of keeping the building in repair. So they decided that the churchwardens must solicit for subscriptions, to be supplemented, if necessary, by an evening collection one Sunday a month, and if the worst came to the worst, every week.

The churchwardens had civil responsibilities, being associated with the Overseer in the relief of the poor, with the Surveyor in the upkeep of roads and with the Constable in the maintenance of order. In Holt (but not everywhere) one churchwarden was chosen by the parson and one by the people. Unlike the other officers of the parish, their appointment was not subject to the approval of the Justices.

The parish was responsible for its destitute, and the

The Special Constable

Vestry fixed the rate. In 1843 it was 8d. in the £, and that
hungry year six single men, one married with a family,
three women and a number of children, sought to emigrate
to the promised land of Canada. The Vestry borrowed
£135 for them, to be repaid out of the poor rate. Like the
other officers, the Overseer of the Poor was unpaid, and had
to serve for a year whether he wanted to or not, but by
this date he had an assistant, who received a small sum for
doing the "donkey" work. In those days, the parish had
to keep up its roads. Work was financed out of a rate,
but originally farmers had to send teams free of charge,
and others were compelled to work for six days a year to
do the job. Stones were extracted from the parish pit, and
the condition of the roads may be imagined !

In 1895, the Vestry minutes shrink to half a page a year,
for the Parish Council had arrived. The old Rector, who
had been in Holt since 1853, signed them with a shaky hand.
The great days of the Vestry Meeting faded out with him.
The parish "in Vestry assembled" disappeared from the
English scene.

*   *   *   *   *

The staff hangs by its cord on the wall. It is 17 inches long,
black, has a crown upon it, and the letters V.R., and a
gilded wooden knob on top ; the symbol of benign
authority, it can surely never have been used to "thack"
a wrong doer. The parish Constable's staff looks just right
in that low room pierced with sunbeams, where there is
always fresh food on the table to welcome the caller. The
staff belonged to the owner's grandfather, James, a mild
man, who was Constable of East Beckham. All the official
work he ever did was to help folk fill in forms, for he was
a good scholar, and in the 'nineties some could neither read
nor write . . . Incidently, he made pills, too, which were
handy for parishioners who did not want a long walk to the
nearest chemist. James was a carpenter, working at Upper
Sheringham ; he went there on foot, carrying half a loaf of
bread soaked in beer, and two red herrings for his sus-
tenance. Yet, even in those days, a constable's life was
not always so free from official bother. At Little Fransham
the constable refused to go to the assistance of the regular
police, and was fined in consequence. There had been a
squabble, and some young fellows had begun fighting.

The constable's job was for centuries an unpopular one,
though of great antiquity and some importance. Perhaps
he originated from the Anglo-Saxon Tithingman, who was
responsible for ten families. Latterly, he was often
appointed by the Magistrates (never by the parish) and had

115

to serve for a year at least. Before the days of regular police, the constable had many duties, and he was lucky if he got any remuneration, even for loss of time. He had to arrest offending persons, keeping them in custody till they could be brought before a magistrate ; make sure that there were no unlicensed inns, faulty weights or measures, or tradesmen following trades without having served proper apprenticeships. He had to go long journeys taking destitute people to the parishes to which they rightly belonged, and which were bound to support them. Ann Sutherland was apprehended at Cobham in Surrey, begging, in October 1781. Her husband had been a legal inhabitant of Holt, so thither she was sent by stages, being escorted by the respective constables of Cobham, St. Magnus, London Bridge, Newmarket, Thetford and Croxton.

A Norfolk constable's expenses in 1833 included "Taking and keeping in hold German, one day and night, eating etc., 5s." He got 2s. and 6d. for seven weeks for "Clearing the parish of Vagrants and other suspicious persons". For apprehending Thomas Butters, and taking him to the Bridewell at Walsingham (about 10 miles) he received 12s. Perhaps a few constables enjoyed the doubtful dignity of office, and the sight of the official staves fixed outside their house-doors (at Walsoken a new staff cost 2s in 1785), but there were sometimes idle and vile persons using slanderous and baleful words to the constable's wife, and even beating the constable himself.

*   *   *   *   *

The coming of the machine age dislocated the life of England. There was unemployment, starvation, crime, and matters were worst in the urban parishes. In 1820 it was said there were more burglaries committed in Norwich in three months than in the previous two decades, yet it was not until sixteen years later that the first regular policeman wearing a dark blue tail coat, waterproof cape, and top hat, appeared in the city. There were only eighteen of them, but before long their numbers were increased, and they were having a rough time of it.

In the 1830s, machine-breaking and stack burning became common in the county. Some farmers got rid of their new "troshing machines" in self-defence. In November 1830, landowners and others in the Melton Constable district called for help as a mob of half-starving men, desperate enough for almost any outrage, were up to mischief. Some gentlemen arrived on horseback, special constables were sworn in, and there was a scuffle at Hindolveston, where the Riot Act was read. The horsemen managed to grab seven or eight rioters, and rode off with them to Walsingham Bridewell. The next day trouble was anticipated, as the prisoners were being taken to Norwich. A message from the High Sheriff at the meet of the Norfolk Foxhounds in North Elmham Park sent a hundred of the followers to Hindolveston, where the prisoners were being charged. In spite of a threatening mob, the captives were held, and an escort of Yeomanry lodged them eventually in Norwich Castle. Detachments of the "1st Royals" were sent to Holt and North Walsham to keep the peace. How maddeningly unfair this show of force must have seemed to people who only craved the means to earn an honest livelihood.

Nine years later, after some opposition, the county magistrates agreed to countenance a regular rural police force. Many parish constables could neither read nor write, and "living amongst friends and relations, and possibly customers, could not be supposed to take measures to prevent crime." So, at last, in 1840, the first 120 policemen were appointed, at wages of £1 per week. There were 12 superintendents with districts of 12 square miles, who got salaries of £100 per annum. The Chief Constable received £500 a year. Still there were not nearly enough policemen to go round, and many parish constables survived. Some members of the present force, in their early years, were contemporary with a few of the original parish constables, who were not finally extinct till 1930.

"The policeman's lot is not a happy one", sings the chorus, yet the regular policeman takes up his career of his own free will—many a parish constable had to serve whether he liked it or not.

*   *   *   *   *

Almost a generation has grown up under the Welfare State. Just as it seemed impossible to believe that the Appointed Day in July 1948 was going to change so many things, so now it is quite difficult to realise how lean and difficult was the time before.

In the 'thirties, the Guardians of the Poor, though they were then officially a Guardians' Committee of the County Council met monthly at the "Institution", which many still called the Workhouse. It was a formidable barrack-like building with ostentatious turrets, set far away in the fields in the 1850s, for the policy of the Poor Law Commissioners was to put their establishments in thoroughly unattractive and lonely situations.

How hated were those Boards of Guardians, established under the Poor Law Amendment Act of 1834! They were

117

elected by the rate-payers, with a sprinkling of magistrates, and it was the farmer-guardians stacks which were burnt first in the early days of acute discontent. Guardians were reviled for their stinginess. The amount of food given to inmates of the new workhouses was less than that allowed to prisoners; perhaps, most unpopular of all, married couples were separated. Outdoor relief was supposed to be withdrawn; in practise this could never be inforced, but the amount given was less than that earned by the lowest paid man in employment. Nevertheless, workhouses were crowded with the destitute, disabled, and infirm, of all ages.

*   *   *   *   *

Mrs. Mary Hewitt was a widow, who found herself in very difficult circumstances, after the death of her husband, and her case was investigated by the Rev. Richard Cobbold, A.M., of Wortham in Suffolk, who later wrote her complete history, which was published in order that she might receive some benefit from its sales. The book's title was *Mary Ann Wellington* and it gives a good idea of the hardness of the times.

The following is an extract from her "history" as described by the Rev. Cobbold:

"Mrs Hewitt, it is especially required, if you can go, that you should appear before the Board of Guardians in person. You have only a moderate distance to go, you must not be afraid."

The widow sighed. She was sad and shrank from parading all her misfortunes and circumstances before these people composing the board.

She thought of the many cases she had known where the poor people had to travel many miles in all weathers. Aged females tramping through the mire and snow, through wind and rain to apply to the Board of Guardians for relief.

There they sat, in one common room with wet shoes and stockings, with clothes drenched through awaiting the summons of the officer to go before the Board. It is true some do not heed it, for there are some people who can feel no degradation; but there is no shame for honest people to stand before the tribunal.

But the poor widow was reduced to the necessity, and she went to the Board of Guardians. She had no alternative but to do so or starve. She sat down amongst numerous other applicants in the common room, till her name was called.

She entered, with a heart beating violently and limbs trembling. As she entered, every eye beheld a tall, straight person, in deep mourning, but with an air of past in-

118

dependence, and a countenance that spoke of much sorrow.

"Walk up here, Mrs. Hewitt," said the Chairman, and then began to question her.

"What is your application here to-day?"

The poor woman stood before the Chairman, the Vice-chairman and a numerous body of Guardians, the Clerk to the Board, the Relieving Officers, and the Governor of the House (workhouse) and had to answer publicly any questions which any man there present choose to put to her.

Severe sometimes are the cross-examinations which an applicant has to undergo, and not always in the gentlest terms; for there sit too often accuser, judge and jury, and the poor creature has little chance of escaping the most vigorous application of the exact letter of the law, but, however, although she was standing there terrified and feeling like a criminal, the Board dealing with her case were composed of kindly people who tried not to deal too harshly with the poor in their day of need. Here are some of the questions they asked the widow:

"What is your name?" "Where do you live?" "What age are you?" "How many children do you have?" "What are your earnings?" What do your children earn?" "How long have you been a widow?" "Have you any pension?" "Have you no means of subsistence?" "Are you able-bodied?" "Have you no friends?" "To what parish did your husband belong?" "How came you to be so reduced?" "Cannot you do something for a livelihood?" "Are you quite destitute?"

She replied that she was the widow of a soldier who had fought through all the peninsular wars and that she had been with him all the time and had stood with the soldiers of her country in the face of England's bitterest and most formidable enemies, but she admitted that she had known no fear until her appearance before the Board.

She was then asked to leave the room for a moment while the Chairman conferred with the Board on the widow's case:

"This is a most extraordinary case," said the Chairman "and her history is remarkable. I have heard, gentlemen, something of her circumstances before, though the woman was personally unknown to me. I have no reason whatever to doubt the facts that she states, and I think some interest should be made to get her case reported to the Government. If we could find someone to report to Her Majesty the condition she is now in, I feel persuaded some relief might be obtained for her. A memorial should be drawn up, either by the civic authorities, or by the woman herself and attested by credible witnesses. At all events the woman is now completely destitute. Every widow should support one child if able-bodied; but I think there are some peculiarities in this case which render her a proper object for the exercise of that privilege which we possess of administering out-door relief. The daughters are of very good character and are working at very respectable houses. The mother and child might be relieved out of doors, and in the meantime I will see some influential friends to see what else can be done for her. What relief shall be given her?"

One suggested a shilling and a stone of flour; and another two-and-sixpence; another two shillings for the mother and one shilling for the daughter.

"Well," said the Chairman, "suppose we give her three shillings? One shilling for the child and two for the mother."

And so it was agreed that she be given three shillings per week for the present.

Later a petition was addresed to Her Majesty the Queen Dowager (Queen Adelaide) by Mrs. Hewitt, the widow in question, as follows:

To Her Majesty the Queen Dowager

"May it please your Majesty to pardon the liberty I have taken in addressing you. I hope your Majesty will not think me incroaching on your goodness in this appealing to you. I am the widow you so kindly relieved last Christmas.

"Through the loss of my husband; who provided for and protected me for forty years, I am worn down with grief and hardship, and do not know what resource to fly to. I have had the painful necessity of applying for parish relief, which has been worse to me than all the hardships endured in the Peninsular wars.

"All they allow me is three shillings per week, for myself and youngest daughter; which has almost driven me to despair.

"I hope your Majesty will be pleased to take my case into your consideration again and the prayers of the widow and orphans will for ever attend you.

"Should your Majesty wish to refer to any gentlemen in the neighbourhood concerning me I beg to mention the Bishop of Norwich, Sir Wm. Foster, Mayor of Norwich, Mr. Freeman, late Mayor; The Rev. J. D. Borton, Rector of Blofield, and the Rev. Mr. Cobbold of Wortham, Nr. Diss. The latter gentleman has kindly consented to publish my history in the hope it may benefit me.

"I remain, your Majesty's Humble Servant,

Mary Hewitt

"Ten Bell Lane, Norwich,
October, 25th, 1845."

120

In due course, a letter was received by all those mentioned in the widow's petition to the Queen Dowager from Marlborough House, London.

*   *   *   *   *

After a further lapse of time, Mary Hewitt received a communication from the Queen Dowager's secretary, stating that Her Majesty had been greatly moved by Mrs. Hewitt's letter and had presented it to some prominent ministers in Parliament. Her case had been discussed and considered to be deserving of help. This, the secretary stated, had been granted and Mrs. Hewitt would receive a small pension for the rest of her life.

Mrs. Hewitt replied, expressing her gratitude at the Dowager Queen's interest in her case and also to all those kindly local gentlemen, whose interest had made the pension possible.

*   *   *   *   *

The Guardians themselves were a cross-section of fairly influential people. As the decades passed, they became more humanitarian. One of them, in the early years of the century, was a tall person who used to walk from his palatial rectory the seven miles to and from the Workhouse—almost as far as the tramps who sought a night's lodging there, after sleeping at the Walsingham House. The doctor at the Workhouse was a sympathetic man, who gossiped endlessly with the inmates, and gave the old people sausages for tea.

By the nineteen thirties' the Guardians' Committee consisted of representatives of local authorities and co-opted members. It sat in a fine high room at the Institution (a more polite name for the Workhouse). There was a big window facing south, and looking over the front door of the building. The Chairman was a tactful woman historian who had occupied that position for years, and meetings were friendly and well-conducted. Two members of the committee used to inspect "The House" in turns, and make a report. With the master and matron (husband and wife) they threaded the incredible labyrinth of deep narrow passages with stone floors. The inmates sat in sparsely furnished rooms, wearing ill-assorted clothes. The only bright thing was the big coal fire which burned behind the guard—so much more cheerful than the invisible heating of to-day. Two callow young Guardians, on their first inspection suggested a number of alterations and improvements, including the use of the board room by residents, except

121

on the monthly meeting day. Their report was listened to politely, but ignored.

By this date the children, mercifully, had been taken from the "Workhouse", and put in an old rectory, in the neighbouring village, under the care of a kind couple. Apart from the main block of the Institution, was the infirmary for the old and bedridden. It was to the credit of the Guardians of former times that, up to 1930, they had administered 94,000 beds for the sick-poor, and the Local Sanitary Authority, which was empowered to do this, had only 40,000, and those mostly for infectious diseases. A proud old woman in the infirmary asked a guardian where she was. "In a Home" was the tactful reply. But a loud voice came from another bed, "That she's not, this is . . . Workhouse."

After the general meetings, the Guardians' Committee split up into two groups, and assisted by the relieving officers, dealt with application for outdoor relief. Half-crowns and small sums were awarded weekly, and "liable relatives" had to be taken into consideration when doing this. The chairman once asked a personal applicant what special expenses he had. "I keeps a bicycle, Sir". The Chairman, a dour Scotsman, was not amused.

Master and Matron of a Workhouse

Many of the guardians arriving in their motor cars (for which no mileage allowance was paid) had deep sympathy for the very poor, but little vision of a different society. To them the immemorial cleavage looked unbridgeable ; some people were ordained to have the whole loaf, and others but the crumbs. Their "Institution" was far better than it had been a generation before, when it was officially a Workhouse. They felt proud of it, as they sat chatting in the sunshine after the meeting.

Then, at last, came the Appointed Day, in 1948, and the Institutions became Hostels in the twinkling of an eye. Some were designated as Hospitals, and some closed their doors for ever. Thus . . . ceased to be. There it stands still, in a countryside little changed in a century. A wit has put up a notice near the gate ". . . Palace". Some parts of the building had been adapted, and are occupied by families. It is a forlorn place, but in spite of all the suffering it has harboured, it stands as a mile-stone on the long road to the Welfare State.

NORFOLK YOUTH

I was born at Kenninghall, in Norfolk, on May 25th, 1890, but was only a year old when my family moved to Palgrave, where my father had taken up an appointment as Farm Steward. As our house was not ready, we spent six miserable months in a tiny cottage; the area was frequented by gypsies, a disorderly law-breaking set of people, including some "Diddicoes", mostly travelling tinkers who lived in caravans but were not gypsies. They were expert thieves; in fact, it had been known for two women to call at a house and, as one of them would be engaging the mistress in conversation, the other would be taking the washing off the line. The gypsies would have nothing to do with them, and fights between the two sections were common. It was a superstition that they could put a spell on cattle or pigs, so if any farm animals died or contracted a disease after a visit it was put down to them. They peddled cottons, threads, candles, and bootlaces, and generally people bought one small item at least to avoid their displeasure.

Child's Push-cart in use in the 1800's

My earliest recollections were of being taken by my mother for an outing in a push-cart—a rather large affair made of wood. I have since wondered how the mothers of the time, in long skirts, managed to push this "chariot" on the very muddy, stony roads. At the time, I was wearing a red and buff outfit, the trousers were kept down by a loop attached and fastened under the boots.

Once when mother took me in my push-cart to Diss to do her shopping we had a frightening experience. There was a feud between two men who lived in the area and clashes between them were frequent. One was a local man, the other being a dealer from just over the border in Suffolk.

It was market day and the town was full of shoppers from the country around. Presently shots were heard and the crowd disappeared, as if by magic, so that the contestants had the Market Place to themselves. After a good deal of manoeuvring in and out of the stalls, the local man managed to disarm his opponent.

The dealer turned and ran for his horse and cart; the local man in close pursuit. He had just reached the vehicle when the dealer savagely beat him with his whip-stalk till finally he had to give up.

One can gather something of the awe in which the local man was held by the fact that, when a fair was held, if he was known to be in the vicinity, the boxing booth would close until he had left the area. Many tales and legends were extant of his prowess as a fighter, for instance one public house "had its counter split right across where he had struck it with his fist; he was said to have fought six Dragoons in the yard of the "Bell Inn", and gave them all a beating".

* * * * *

Whenever we, who lived at Palgrave in Suffolk wanted to visit Diss, in Norfolk, it was necessary to pass through an area on the outskirts of the town known as "Denmark". Many of the roughest characters resided on Fair Green, in 2-roomed cottages of lath, and plaster, with rents of only 2s. to 3s a week. There were some who were always behind with their payments, but most landlords were very considerate and did not press the matter too far. They led a hand-to-mouth existence, it was almost a question of survival of the fittest. The children who survived were generally "tough" and had a lot of stamina. Once, when my friend and I were crossing the bridge over the river, we were confronted by a couple of hefty lads, who said "Where

125

do you think you're going?" We replied "Into the town, as far as the Coffee Tavern." "We don't know so much about that" said the lads. Whereupon we struck out, each taking his man, and dashed off, dodging down some passages and by-roads to shake off our pursuers. Similar incidents occurred all the time, and if you should live in Suffolk and have a girl friend in Norfolk, you would be warned to seek one elsewhere. There would be no second warning, and you would have to fight your way out of the town or village concerned next time such an occasion occurred.

There were army manœuvres on the commons and heaths nearby, and sometimes units would lie in camp for a month or more during the summer . . . Many a soldier married a local girl. One farmer's daughter married a Captain of the "Scots Greys". The farmer laid on a magnificent reception—marquees and everything. A baker and confectioner in Diss did the catering, and it was voted a great success, until the farmer received the bill. He kept the caterer waiting so long before he paid the account that he nearly put the man out of business. The farmer, too, took a long time to get clear of all the expense incurred.

When I was still young my mother took me to see the circus procession through Diss. On one of the decorated vehicles was a lady impersonating "Britannia", with a *real* lion at her feet. Everybody was very thrilled to see the lion lying so quietly on the top of the circus wagon. When the procession arrived on the ground where all the vans were parked, the lion walked about half way down the steps from the tall van, jumped on to the ground, and ran around several times before it was caught. Someone shouted "The lion is loose" and, on hearing this, my mother lost no time in getting me home in the push-cart. The lion was an old one and not at all dangerous, but a lion was a lion to country people!

*   *   *   *   *

My school days were interrupted by a year at home suffering from the effects of bronchitis, so my sister taught me to read and write, and gave me lessons in simple arithmetic. Therefore, I skipped the Primary Classes, and commenced my school life in Standard I. They were happy days, with games in which the master took part—football, hockey, cricket, paper-chasing, etc. When the village pond was frozen over for long periods there was plenty of skating and sliding. One day, the Master was doing some rather fancy movements, when he fell, and the ice broke. As he

126

cut a sorry figure emerging from the water, some of the boys laughed, and were reported to the Headmaster by his wife. Later, they were escorted to the Headmaster's room, where punishment was duly carried out. Every Monday morning the Rector would call at the school and take the "assembly". I well remember the ritual. "Good morning children", and our reply "Good morning, Sir." He was a bearded man and had a benevolent appearance, but this was misleading. He could be very autocratic, and, on occasions, very overbearing. If you attended church you shared in any benefits which might be going, if you were not a church member you were out of luck when it came to winter-time, and the bequests of coal, which should have been given to all aged people of 70 and over, just didn't come your way. Also, I remember, that one day, whilst returning from school, we were looking for beech-nuts on the bank of a meadow which belonged to Miss Kay, a very nice lady, who always waved to us boys when she passed in her carriage ; on this occasion when His Reverence was passing in his gig, with coachman behind, he leaned out and lashed us with his whip. My friend, who was a giant for his age, was mad with rage and ran behind the gig shaking his fist and calling the Parson all the names in the calendar. I thought we should have heard more of this, but, fortunately for us, the Reverend Gentleman couldn't have heard. The Parson was a power in the village, and all males had to "touch their caps" to him ; also all women and girls had to curtsey, calling him all sorts of names after he had passed by!

The head boy of the school used to decide what punishment should be meted out to a junior who had been rude to a senior. There was "running the gauntlet of fire and water" ; two ranks of boys faced inwards, and the offender had to run up and down the line three times. If it was "fire" the culprit would be belaboured with knotted handkerchiefs, if "water" was chosen, all the boys would spit at the unfortunate one—a very unpleasant ordeal. If a quarrel broke out between two boys, they were hustled into a circle with boys all round, and had to fight it out and fair play was ensured by the head boy. It was a rough life really.

On the farm, in our leisure hours, the horse-play and other things we did all helped to shape us for adult life. Driving cattle to market and from the train ; exercising one of the ponies with a halter, and a blanket to sit on, a very precarious seat as I often found before becoming proficient.

127

The countryman is always portrayed as a "Bumpkin", an ignorant clot, but they liked nothing better than to have a "Towny" staying on the farm, so that they could show him a few things. The Towny would be asked to assist in catching some young owls. His job would be to hold a sieve, using a two-tined fork, up against the slatted aperture at the top of the stable wall, to prevent the owls getting out, whilst the farm boys would go up the ladder inside the stable to collect the owls with a sack. The farm boys also carried a pail of water to the loft, and called out "Are you ready?" Back came the reply, "Yes", and then the Towny received a shower of water, soaking him to the skin.

When I was 13, my friend, the schoolmaster's son sat for a scholarship, and later attended Eye Grammar School. I had been receiving instruction with Harry with a view to taking the exam. too, but my father said it was more important to have a trade. One didn't argue with one's parents in those days, and I was apprenticed to a firm of Printers, called Messrs. Lusher Brothers. They told my father they would make a tradesman of me, and they taught me everything they knew. The first year I was a "Printer's Devil". In the winter months it was very trying. The first duty was to take down the shutters, and light the "Tortoise" stoves. Cinders had to be sifted, and hods of coke filled. Nothing could be printed until the works were warm enough for the ink to move freely on the composition rollers. All this, and cleaning the machines and rollers and gas engine made the Printer's Devil very dirty with ink stains on his face and hands. I had also to run errands, and deliver printed work to customers. It has often been said that "a woman's work is never done", and it was the same with the Printer's Devil.

In the second year I became a slightly superior person, receiving some instruction in the art of printing and by the end of the final year, could operate any machine in the works—a very comprehensive education. I experienced many amusing incidents. Once, at election time, I had to take proofs to the agent of the Unionist party. My masters were Liberals and Non-conformists, but they printed for both sides, in red ink for the Unionists or Torys, and in blue for the Liberals. The agent laid the poster proof out on the table, and read the words on the bill for my benefit. "Vote for Mann (the Tory) printed by a couple of damn good Liberals."

Every morning at eleven o'clock the senior partner of the printing works would call up the tube to the composing room "Lunch!" and the entire works would stop for a ten-minute break. The management would go down to the cellar and return with a bottle of stout which was placed by

128

the stove in winter to warm it up a bit. One morning, when the bottle of stout was unscrewed and poured out, it was found to contain nothing stronger than water. The two Lusher brothers were furious ; finally, they sent for the "Printer's Devil", gave him the stout bottle with the water in it, and told him to go and see the manager of the brewery, and tell him that Messrs. Lusher Brothers sent their respects, and would like to know how it was that he had filled one of the stout bottles with water. The manager was annoyed, and told the boy it was impossible for his machines to fill a bottle with water, and that Messrs. Lusher Brothers should look a little nearer home for the explanation of the affair. So the staff was called together and questioned. The last to be asked was John Nice, who admitted responsibility, and got a good ticking off, but it was quite an occasion.

*　　*　　*　　*　　*

At the termination of my apprenticeship as a printer at Diss, I was offered a job as compositor by Fletcher and Son Ltd. of Castle Works in Davy Place at Norwich, and was driven to the station to catch the train by my friend. I knew I should miss him, and I believe he felt the same about me. After I had settled in Norwich he did visit me now and then, and we never lost touch, even though he went to Australia.

Arriving at Norwich I felt completely overawed by all the hustle and traffic. Leaving my trunk at the station, I made my way to Fletchers, where I met the managing director, Mr. Mason. He was a very nice, fatherly type of man and, seeing I was nervous, put me at my ease at once by a remark which allayed all my fears. After a chat about the work I should be doing, he introduced me to Mr. Turner, one of the Composing room staff, who, he thought, might be able to help me in the matter of accommodation. This was providential, as I had made no arrangements for lodgings, and this man took me to see his mother, and we fixed up things very agreeably, and I stayed there until I joined the army in August, 1914. The date was now November 9th, 1909. Mrs. Turner and her husband were good Methodist people; they took me with them to church every Sunday, and later introduced me to some of the young men there, who were full of life and high spirits, and we had a lot of fun together.

It was not long before we started a physical culture club in a room over a fish shop in Dereham road. The shop-keeper was an ex-sailor, and did a lot for us, especially with

129

installing the equipment for our use. Then we formed a football club which was in being till the war broke it up, most of its members joining the Forces. Boating and swimming were other pursuits, and in the summer we would often walk down to the "Eagle" and have a dip about 6 a.m.

One of the members of our "crowd" was Ernest Faircloth, and I became especially attached to him and, living in the same street, we were in close touch. He was an artist apprentice with Page Bros., Back St. Stephens Street, Norwich. This was the same firm where A. J. Munnings, the well-known artist, served his apprenticeship, and Ernest worked at the same bench which Munnings had used earlier. Munnings was a great inspiration to young students at the Norwich Art School in St. George's Street.

This was a time when the only picture show in Norwich was at Victoria Hall, St. Stephen's Street, and the charge was 2d. There was a man in a bowler hat standing just at the entrance, announcing the titles of films, and, apparently, there was one continuous performance, for whenever one went by, he was always saying "Now Showing". It was a poor show, and one can understand why the name "flicks" caught on ; the best seats were just bare forms, and the rest of the audience stood about in groups. It was quite a relief to get out into the air again, as there was a lot of smoking.

Roller skating was very much the vogue at this time, and the "rinkeries" were on the corner where "Delves Motors" building now stands, with dancing nightly to the music of the "Blue Hungarian" band. There were also attractive programmes at the Hippodrome and Theatre. Trams had just been introduced, and there was only an odd car or two in use, and everyone raced off the road if one of these appeared in sight. Hansom cabs and "flys" were still plying for hire, and both had their "ranks" about the city. In summer the "Jenny Lind" paddle-steamer made daily trips to Bramerton "Woods End", and Coldham Hall, and there were concert parties at "The Nest" football ground, Spring Gardens, and the Gardens in Thorpe.

The Norfolk Agricultural Show was held at Crown Point, Whitlingham, in June, 1911, and King George V and Queen Mary visited Norwich. There was a grand parade in the city when the King rode at the head of the Royal Norfolk Yeomanry in their attractive uniforms. It was a great day for Norwich ; Ailwyn Fellowes was knighted by King George in St. Andrew's Hall. Sir Ailwyn lived at Honingham Hall, which was entirely demolished by contractors in 1966. All that perpetuates its memory is a small, ancient building which has been restored to its original condition.

Early on a Sunday morning one could lie in bed and hear the calls of different street salesmen who went from house to house loudly proclaiming their particular speciality. There was the deep, throaty voice of the man selling "fine kippered herrin' ", closely followed by the fellow with the high-pitched voice calling out "fine pink shrimps". Then the short, sharp cry of the milkman, and sometimes an astonishing call from a man pushing an old wheelbarrow, closely followed by his daughter ; they went from door to door with a basket of cockles. The old man stopped now and then, put down his barrow, took a deep breath, and then let out the most ear-splitting yell of "Cockles, a-l-i-v-e!".

In the city were flower-sellers on the "Walk", and a character named Billy Bluelight who used to roam the streets day and night, calling out "Mr. Leech's Cough Remedy". This was produced by a Great Yarmouth chemist, and was very popular. Billy Bluelight was a great runner, and is reputed to have run the whole distance from Yarmouth to Norwich, arriving on the Norwich City football ground at half-time.

The city was full of strange characters. There was an odd-job man called "Sugar-me-Sop", and the legendary figure of Spring-heeled Jack, who was said to possess some wonderful shoes which gave him the power to spring long distances. His speciality was to jump from "nowhere at all" down into the midst of card-players seated on the ground on Mousehold Heath ; before they had time to recover from their surprise, Spring-heeled-Jack would snatch all the money from the "kitty" and disappear with one of his gigantic springs. Mothers used to warn their children to watch out for Spring-heeled-Jack when they went to play on Mousehold. Then there was a woman named Maggie Murphy, a street singer, who sang as she marched along in a pair of men's boots. She was followed by a crowd of jeering kids. Her speciality was hymn tunes, and sometimes she would stop her singing and call out to the children "Clear off you little B - - - - 's" and so on. She was often "run in" for causing a public mischief.

There was also a curious character with a withered arm, who used to stand outside some of the large stores, singing, and moving from place to place, until the traders could not stand it any longer, and an order was passed prohibiting him from singing in Norwich.

Another regular performer was the tin-whistle player, whose pitch on Thursdays was near the "Red Lion" in Castle Street. Some went as far as to pay him well for "clearing off". Once, whilst walking down the Guildhall Hill, I saw a large crowd at the bottom round a frightened young woman, who was wearing a harem suit—a very comfortable affair with Turkish trousers. The girl would presently have been in some danger from a threatening crowd, but the police arrived and put the "daring" young lady into a hansom cab, and sent her home.

*   *   *   *   *

On August Bank Holiday, 1914, I went to Yarmouth with several other young men, as this was our custom. But, on this occasion the day was completely ruined by the tense feeling which prevailed. Territorial troops and Reserves were marching to a camp at Caister-on-Sea, and a martial atmosphere pervaded the whole town. When we returned to Thorpe Station, Norwich, there were soldiers on guard with fixed bayonets at all the exits, which tended to make everyone feel most depressed. The atmosphere of war seemed everywhere, and presently Germany invaded Belgium, and we were in it. Our Expeditionary Force was sent out, and was soon in action, but only just escaped annihilation at Mons ; it reformed, and, with the French, managed to hold the German advance. The Government called for volunteers, and although most people had the idea that the war would be over in a month, it never looked like that to me.

When the eight of us next met, I said I was joining the army. If any of them decided to do the same, I would meet them at the corner of Rampant Horse Street at 2 p.m. on the 10th August. Only one turned up, and we proceeded to the examination centre in St. Andrew's Hall, and were told to report at Britannia Barracks on Mousehold on the 22nd of the month where we were to be attested by Major B. W. A. Keppel of Weston Old Hall, near Norwich and became from that time "D" Company of the 8th Battalion the Norfolk Regiment. On that occasion, Sidney Page and I stood in the ranks with a young man who was to be our friend and companion all through the conflict— "Jimmy" Smith. A real "comrade" in good times and bad.

We all entrained at Thorpe Station next morning for Shorncliffe Camp in Kent. Arriving there about 4 p.m. we were supplied with a tent for every 12 men. As we were sitting down, someone opened the flap of the tent, and a large tin of plum and apple jam was rolled in, followed by four loaves of bread. This was our ration for the remainder of that day. We were still in our "civvy" clothes, and we wore them until well into November. When it became colder, we had to send home for our overcoats, and were credited with £1 each for these.

132

Next morning, after a cup of tea and a biscuit at the Y.M.C.A., we had to fall in for a bathing parade. We marched all the way to Sandgate, a distance of about four miles, and enjoyed a swim in the sea. One fellow ran into trouble by losing his false teeth when he was caught off-balance by a large wave. Then we went back to breakfast at camp, and had only our small pocket knives to eat porridge and bacon with. After breakfast, it was platoon drill until 12.30; lunch at 1 p.m., after which we were taken for a long march and to do some field training. As we had no equipment to carry or rifles, it was quite enjoyable. In the evenings we would go to Folkestone for a show. Luckily we had taken a little money with us, as we were not paid for a month. We had been at Shorncliffe about a month, when Lord Kitchener came to review the troops, but we did not see him as we had no uniforms, and we were taken well away on a kind of exercise-cum-picnic, so that he should not see us in our shabby civilian attire, looking for all the world like some broken-down South American "guerillas". However, the weather was beautiful until it broke late one night with a fearful gale and heavy rain-storm. Our tent pole broke in half, and the wet canvas dropped on the twelve of us. We spent the rest of the night in a large marquee, with a lot of "Old Sweats" who were grumbling about "blinking Rookies" disturbing their night. There must have been some small airships at Dover about this time ; we often saw them on the distant skyline, but were unable to get a close view.

In early November we entrained for Colchester, and entered the Meeanee Barracks there ; we took over from a regular regiment which had been ordered abroad. Knowing that we were "Rookies", I often wondered if, before the soldiers moved out, they had left a "small" surprise for us. At this time there were fires in the barrack-room ; one night, after we were asleep, there was an explosion up the chimney, and the room seemed full of smoke. My friends and I were on some trestles near the chimney, and wondered if the explosion was due to enemy action, but then we found some exploded bullets in the fireplace which must have been left by the former occupants.

Our platoon commander was a nice young man, and the nephew of a famous general, but he was also the most excitable person I ever met, especially on field days. He was always in trouble with Captain North, our Company Commander, as he never completely mastered all the intricacies of military drill on the square or during cere-monial exercises.

133

COLCHESTER BOMBED BY GERMAN AIRCRAFT

WHILST we were in the Meeanee Barracks in Colchester, there was an explosion in the night. A German "Taube" aeroplane had dropped the first bomb ever to fall in this country. It caused a direct hit on the Cavalry Barracks, and some soldiers were wounded. After that, there were many raids by "Zeppelins", and a lot of damage was caused in all parts of the country, including London.

When our first uniform was issued to us it consisted of a blue blouse and slacks, with a field service cap. We were almost ashamed to appear in public wearing these awful uniforms. One day we went (Jim, Sid, and I) to London to visit my friend, Ernest, who was an artist with Waterlows the printers. We all went to Lyons' "Corner House" restaurant in Oxford Street, where we had lunch. Whilst there we suffered the final shame of being taken for Belgian refugees !

When we arrived, after "lights out", at our barracks that night, and opened the door to enter, a loaf of bread hit us amidships, and this puzzled us, but it transpired that a half-pound of margarine had been placed in the bed of one, Hugh Palmer, so that when he laid down on it the greasy mess spread all over his blankets. Hugh was a Norfolk farmer from Kenninghall, and thinking that it was the culprit coming into the room who had commited this outrage, let fly with the loaf. The culprit is rarely found out when he perpetrates a joke on his fellow-men because no-one would give him away.

Some time after that, Hugh tried to get leave to go home to sort things out for his wife, who was managing the farm in his absence, but was refused permission. So he approach me with a proposition. He would take out a late night pass and go home, and would I kindly hand it in at the guard room when I returned to Barracks? Being of the same build, he said, it shouldn't be difficult if I took care not to show myself too much at the guard-room door. He would return on the Sunday night, and no-one would know anything about it. Schemes never turn out as planned, and this was no exception. Early on Sunday morning, we opened up Hugh's bed, and left it unmade. When the orderly sergeant went the rounds, he was told that Palmer had gone to the latrines. He seemed to accept that, but later in the morning he came round again and said "Palmer back yet?" And we replied "Not yet ! " Then he went into the attack again, employing rather different methods. He said, "We know that Palmer is absent, and also that someone handed his late-night pass in for him. Another thing, we know who he is, so it is up to that man to own up and tell us all he knows before he runs into further trouble." Then the sergeant left again.

Everybody knew that I had handed in the pass, but I was advised to say nothing about it. There was a lot going on, but I just kept silent on the matter, and the act the sergeant had put on was one big bluff. Palmer did not come back on the Sunday night, but arrived about the middle of Monday morning, so he was really for the "high jump". There was a further questioning about the late-night pass which I had handed in, and the whole affair ended, but, of course, Palmer had to appear before the C.O. and explain his action, but he didn't get anything worse than a few days confined to barracks, coupled with fatigue duties after parade, commonly known as "jankers".

*   *   *   *   *

Whilst we were at Colchester, we enjoyed ourselves when off duty, which was in the evenings. Our days were fully occupied for His Majesty all the time we were at this military town. Over 20,000 men were living in barracks, hutments, and billeted in houses in the area. We spent half our time on manœuvres in the country round about, taking haversack rations with us, and arriving home about 4 in the afternoon. We were out in the fresh air, and had really enjoyable, but hard, times. Sometimes the Colonel would ask me to hold his horse for him, when he would go to a distant ridge and look at the "enemy" positions through his field glasses. When he returned he would often give me an apple. Colonel Briggs was a nice fatherly old man, and knew just how to treat young soldiers. He was much respected and so was our company commander, Captain North, who, by the way, had a nice daughter much admired by the rank and file. Later, we had to take a firing course on the Middlewick range and were allowed to sit around and smoke until it came to our turn to do the firing. Whilst we were sitting there chatting away, a young officer came along with a squad of men, and seemed unable to get them into the position he had in mind, and was getting hot and bothered. We quietly took the "mickey", and he must have reported it to our captain, who sent our platoon officer along to give us platoon drill until we were wanted on the range ; that took the smile off our faces !

On Saturday mornings we were always employed on coal fatigue, taking our coal buckets (2 men to a bucket) to the coal yard where first of all, we had to take supplies to our officers' quarters. All the men carrying officers' coal made

135

a point of passing by their own quarters with the coal. A man would be waiting at one of the downstair windows, and a few large lumps were given to him as the coal-carriers passed by, for later use in the barrack-room stove.

Later, we had a forced march to Clacton-on-Sea, about 14 miles from Colchester, and a large number of fellows dropped out, so it was decreed that we must have a lot more "endurance" marches. Our next effort was a march in which the whole 18th Division took part, complete with field kitchens, and the headquarters personnel. Our destination was very "hush-hush" and some of us wondered if, ultimately, we should find ourselves on Southampton docks, ready to embark for France, but the time was not yet.

At 8 o'clock one morning we marched away with all our equipment, full pack, everything. It was early spring, and quite warm, and it wasn't long before we began to feel really "whacked". But we kept on, with a ten-minute rest each hour, until at about 3 in the afternoon, we found ourselves on the outskirts of Ipswich. When we reached the Woodbridge road, billeting parties went round the streets commandeering accommodation for a short stay of eight hours. We were due to move off at 11 p.m. that night. The next day we marched to Woodbridge, stayed a fews hours there, and then went on (about 27 miles) to a wild desolate place called Hollesley Bay. We stayed there in isolated barns, farm buildings, etc., for a week, during which time extensive divisional manœuvres took place, night and day. There were no exceptions, everyone had to take part. Sick men had medicine and duty, so everyone really got "sorted out". We slept rough all the time, and the nights were mighty cold, as we had only our great-, coats to keep us warm.

Then came the journey back, marching along dusty roads, there was no tarmac in those days. Suddenly we would have to leave the road and deploy over the adjoining fields to counter an enemy attack. When the enemy retired we would have to form up on the road again, very exhausting work. After we had passed through Woodbridge again we were very tired, and just marched doggedly along without any feeling or interest in anything, but the thought of a good lay-in when we got back to barracks, spurred us on.

*   *   *   *   *

In Camp at Codford. When we arrived back at the barracks in Colchester the air was full of rumours—"we were to proceed overseas, we were destined for the Middle

136

East, we were going to India". All proved to be false, as in a few days we were on our way to a camp at Codford in Wiltshire, chalk soil, and very poor, hill country. The excess of chalk in the water caused an epidemic of diarrhoea amongst the troops. Then, later, two men from our hut were taken to hospital with meningitis. We thought it was very probable we should get it, and, really were prepared for this to happen.

One morning I awoke feeling very queer, with stiffness on each side of my neck ; I thought "this is it!" However, on examination by the doctor, he said "You have mumps, You will have to be isolated for a fortnight, and I was removed to a bell tent on the edge of a wood, nearly all my meals being left a short distance away for me to fetch. The weather was fine and very warm and, altogether, after the first day, I enjoyed myself, and when I waved to my friends marching past with full packs, they used to shake their fists at me. A number of men had very severe attacks, and it transpired that an N.C.O., who had been visiting a family in a nearby village, had brought the infection to our camp.

It was now so hot that we were issued with shorts and sun flaps for our hats. To make things worse, we spent the rest of the time at Codford in large scale manoeuvres, running and attacking up hill and down, sometimes the exercise taking us as far as Gillingham in Dorsetshire, all very exhausting in the extreme heat. It was quite a common thing for fellows to fall down on their faces from heat and exhaustion.

Then we went on our last leave before going overseas (June 1915) and several were in trouble from overstaying their leave. Afterwards we spent some time on coal fatigue at Warminster station, coming back looking like sweeps. After a week-end pass to Southampton, my friend found it was only a matter of days before we set sail, and there was great activity everywhere. We all had to have different inoculations (we had already been vaccinated) and were issued with all sorts of different things, and everybody had to be close-cropped.

*   *   *   *   *

EMBARKING FOR FRANCE

WE WENT down to Folkestone and boarded ship about midnight. The moon was shining bright, and the journey over was very enjoyable. The sea was calm and we sang to the accompaniment of mouth organs. We also ate some of the cakes which had been sent to us earlier. Arriving at Boulogne at about 2 a.m., we disembarked, and were met by crowds of French civilians going to the quay. Some girls were selling biscuits and oranges. A French sentry on guard over some buildings was leaning on a long rifle in a very casual manner, and I said to my friend "Jim, I believe we've lost this war." Our destination was a large area called Saint Martin's Plain, and it was full of bell tents. We had to draw bedding and blankets on our arrival, and it was not long after we had settled down that we were itching all over. This was when we had our issue (with the bedding) of "chats" or lice. I would never have thought it possible for a person to become "lousy" in a matter of minutes. Alas, we were never free from them all the time we were in France !

*   *   *   *   *

Next day French prostitutes were on the move, and Mounted Military Police were on duty all the time chasing them away from the camp. Another thing that had to be seen to be believed was that Sidney and I were told to report to the Y.M.C.A. tent for duties, and found we had to don a white apron, and serve tea, coffee, and cakes, all day. This was O.K. with us, as we had some jolly exciting meals whilst we were there.

Then came the journey up the line. We marched down to Boulogne station. This was very different to an English railway station. Every time a train arrived or departed it seemed as if all the staff went mad, such excitement, blowing of whistles and horns, I had never witnessed the like anywhere before. When we did get going, we only went short distances, and then stopped. This happened all the way to Amiens. Some of the stops were so long one could get out and buy a bottle of wine, and then, with a short run, catch the train again. From Amiens we marched to Molliecourt, where we had billets in some farm premises. From the loft above, we could see the town of Albert with the ruined tower of the cathedral in the sunshine. It was a beautiful view, and it seemed such a pity that the place was so knocked about.

Whilst we were at this farm the occupant was arrested for waving a lighted lantern from the loft window of his barn, and was marched off by troops with fixed bayonets. There were quite a number of traitors arrested from time to time.

When we arrived in the town of Albert we found the damage far worse than we had thought. Most of the factory area was completely destroyed. In one place a bicycle and tyre factory had received a direct hit, scattering

138

bicycles and tyres in all directions, and they had just remained so. A fair complete with stalls, sideshows, and swing boats, was standing in an empty space, looking as if it had been functioning when everybody had to leave in a hurry.

Our first time in the line was at La Boisselle, where on our first night, the Jerrys dropped some "coal boxes"* nearby just to celebrate our arrival. The next day one of our number was blown off the firestep by a shell, and was taken away with severe shell-shock ; also a young sentry, ignoring advice, to "keep his head down", had his brains blown out with an explosive bullet, another fell asleep at his post and was severely reprimanded. All this was due to lack of experience, and, as time went on, one became danger-conscious, and it was almost unheard of for anyone to fall asleep on sentry duty. In this sector of the line we spent many weary months, in and out, with all the monotony of trench warfare, stand-to night and morning, intermittent shell fire, trench mortar fire, (minnenwerfer) another Jerry horror weapon, and in the winter the everlasting mud and cold. Some parts of the line were knee-deep in water all winter. Then there was sentry-go on the firestep, two hours on and four off, sapping down the mine shafts, 30 ft. under the ground, with the Royal Engineers. After ten days we would be relieved and go back to the town of Albert, from where we made nightly visits to the line carrying rations and munitions. We even dug gun pits for the artillery.

One of our colleagues, Fred Burton, was asked to form a drum-and-fife band when we were out of the line, and I said to him playfully "Don't forget me, Fred, when you form your band." I promptly forgot my foolish remark until one day when I was "on-sentry" in the line, a "runner" from Battalion Headquarters arrived and said I was to report immediately to the band sergeant. This really shook me, but I was hoping my small knowledge of music, coupled with a natural aptitude to pick things up quickly would see me through. I shall never forget the look on "Uncle J's" face the first time he saw me marching down the French village street, "playing" an F flute. As I approached he just put his hand over his eyes and shook with laughing. Later, I had to call on my natural ability still further, when they formed a brass band, and I was presented with a "flugal horn"—an instrument which added tone and mellowness to the cornets—I hope ! There were

---

* "Coal boxes" were named thus on account of the noise they made when exploding, and were sent over by a mine-thrower. The German name was "Minnenwerfer".

139

compensations in being a bandsman, one was excused duties in the line at first, so that one could become proficient. The band was often threatened by soldiers resting because the practises disturbed their rest. Even one of my friends said "Bill, if you play that darned thing again when I'm having a sleep, I'll shoot you."

*   *   *   *   *

The day arrived when I came home on leave for ten days. The sea was very rough, and we suffered with seasickness all the way over. Arriving in London, we felt we could have eaten a horse, but when we got to Lyons Café we found there was nothing on the menu but vegetable pie. We had two each of these uninteresting items, and went on our way to Liverpool Street Station. Arriving at Thorpe Station, Norwich, about 2 a.m., we made our way to our seperate places of abode. I just had my old lodgings to go to, and was thankful to lie down and feel safe once again.

The next day I called on my wife to be, and we both went on a round of visits and entertainments. The cold wind had blown all day, and now it was snowing hard, and thus it continued for the whole ten days, and was still cold with wintry showers on the day I returned, with a cake and other goodies in my haversack. Arriving at Southampton, there was a gale blowing, and instead of boarding ship we had to spend the night in sheds at Southampton Docks, as it was too rough for the old tramp steamer to put to sea. A real blizzard was raging in the Channel, and it was two days and nights before we set out from Southampton. On reaching the "Roads" we were wirelessed to return again. It was another 24 hours before we were finally allowed to proceed. Even with these so-called "better" conditions it was the roughest time I had ever spent on a vessel at sea. There was a blizzard still raging, and the ship kept rising on a huge wave ; the next moment it would be going down, down, down, until one wondered if it could ever rise again. I was placed on deck, on submarine duty, and in order to stop myself being washed overboard, had to put my arm through an iron stanchion on deck. It took fourteen hours before we sighted the snow-clad cliffs of Boulogne. Never was a man so relieved to see the sight of land. I was going out to war once more, but even the prospect of that seemed more tolerable than being buffeted by those angry seas, so on putting my feet on the ground I experienced a great feeling of relief. The luckiest people on the ship were a couple of drunken Scotchmen who had been carried on board at Southampton, and had not known a thing about the rough crossing.

140

When the leave party arrived back, the Battalion were on rest at Etinheim, near Bray-sur-Somme, and this was a nice little village where the people and troops got on very well together It was while we were at this place that we had to take over a sector of the front line at a place called Maricourt. Here the line was only about 20 yards from Jerry's, and one had to be very careful not to expose oneself. One good thing, we did not get much shell fire in the front line because of the closeness, but mortar fire and hand grenades were frequent. When we were relieved we only returned to some more trenches (reserve) about 300 yards away.

However, we were only there for a few days, when we were told we were going back to a small village the other side of Amiens. There were a lot of rumours current, but nothing authentic about our "rest" behind the lines.

*   *   *   *   *

PREPARING FOR THE FIRST OF JULY, 1916

IT WAS a long march to Amiens, but I shall never forget the welcome we received. The whole population were lining the streets and, when our band started to play a gay tune, the excitement of these French people overflowed and everyone mingled with troops and we were presented with apples and pears and managed to take a quick drink of wine in our passage through the city. It was a wonderful experience.

The small village which was to be our "home" for about two months was a most picturesque little place and we all "took to it" at once. On arrival, we had a short talk by the Colonel and it was then that we were told we were to have a long period of intensive field training, during which our tactics would consist, mostly, of Open Warfare, as opposed to trench warfare. It was lovely May weather and, though the training was arduous, it was much enjoyed. We also had the luxury of a hot bath now and then.

After a long spell of trench warfare, with its monotonous and dreary routine and continous day-to-day casualties, this small village was *heaven*. About the middle of June, replacements of men from England, started to arrive. This in turn gave rise to all sorts of rumours which were, according to military parlance, "straight from the horses mouth"—the Colonel told his horse, the horse told the groom and he passed the news on to us. A very simple procedure.

After this training, we marched to a small town in the battle area called Bray-sur-Somme ; here the military

141

activity was on a scale, never before seen by our Division. There were French, Indian and British, combined with Colonial troops from many countries. We realised a big battle was imminent. A day or two later a terrific bombardment of the German lines began and continued for a fortnight. Things were very rough, with the German retaliatory artillery fire going on all the time. The noise was deafening.

*   *   *   *   *

We were now digging assembly trenches and suffered many casualties during this operation, but "the show" had to go on. We were now told that the first of July was "the day", and on the morning of the "first" about 5 a.m., troops were on the move everywhere and by 6.30 a.m. we were in the assembly trenches. Everything was very tense and one kept hearing remarks such as "We're only here for life!" and "How long is duration?"

Then came the order to "go over" Everything had been planned, but things did not go according to plan—mines timed to blow-up one minutes before our troops went over the top, did not explode until our men were on the top of the mined area so that numerous men were killed and wounded before the advance really began.

We were in the bombers and the last to go over, so we missed this holocaust. Our job was to "winkle-out" Jerrys who were still sheltering in the dug-outs. They were reluctant to come out, having been told that the British shot all German prisoners. This was entirely wrong, of course, so we often had to call to them and threaten to throw a bomb down if they didn't come out. I cannot remember having any food all day; only water now and then.

One Jerry strong point held out against many attacks, but eventually, we had to send for a Stokes gun battery which soon brought them out with their hands up. Next followed a great tragedy, "Montaubon Alley" a strongly fortified German trench, refused to surrender and the commander of our troops sent a message back asking for artillery support, but no response came from the artillery, so a final onslaught was made and the trench taken. Almost at the moment of occupation by our troops, our artillery put down a devastating "barrage" on the trench, causing havoc amongst those who had just taken it.

We spent the rest of the day as carrying parties for the advancing troops and lost a large number of men, killed and wounded, in passing along a sunken road, which was

142

continually strafed by German shell fire. Coming back from one of these excursions I must have taken a wrong turning in the "maze" of trenches and completely lost my way. Time after time I passed the same two dead bodies lying in the trench.

It had been a hard day, without food, and I suddenly felt exhausted, having walked many miles trying to find a way out. It was now quite dark and impossible to find ones way over the top, so I sat down and waited, hoping someone would come along. Finally, a young officer in the "Suffolks" came along with two men and they directed me back to my base.

My friends were all very relieved to see me, thinking I must have "stopped one". They were in the middle of a welcome meal and I very heartily joined them.

*   *   *   *   *

Next day, our relief arrived and our unit went back for a rest to Bray-sur-Somme for a few days. Two or three days later we had to go back and retake Delville Wood which the Jerry's had recaptured. After a briefing, we went over the top at 6.30 a.m., having to climb over a large number of dead bodies to advance.

The Corporal and Sergeant were killed at the moment of entry into the wood, the victims of some Jerry snipers in the treetops. They were soon brought down and we advanced in the face of heavy fire from artillery and small arms. As we approached the opposite side of the wood, two German soldiers came towards us with their hands up. One was a mere boy of 18 ; the other was a big red-haired soldier, whose appearance may have rather frightened one of our younger soldiers, who, without any hesitation, started to fire at them. I shouted to him to stop firing.

At the same time I ran to the German prisoners and found the young man severely wounded in the wrist. Binding up his wound, he kept saying "Kamerad" to me all the while. I was suddenly conscious that all rifle fire had ceased, and wondered if it was just coincidence, or a sporting gesture by the enemy. Pressing on to the edge of the wood, we tried to dig ourselves in, but there were too many tree roots and no other cover at all, so we were in a very exposed position, holding on, as we had been told reinforcements would arrive. None ever did, until by 6 p.m. there were just two of us left out of seventy men. We were faint and hungry and thought we would have some food (biscuits and cheese) from our haversacks. That was the last thing we ever did in that situation. A sniper blew

143

my companions brains out and I had a bullet through my nose. On my way back (alone), four of our men, thinking I was a Jerry in British uniform, told me to put my rifle down, but I refused and told them what I thought of them. On to the dressing station and six miles down the sunken road to the field hospital.

I had more than a dozen near-misses on the way. One, dropped not more than a yard away and I was just waiting for the explosion, when I suddenly realized it was a dud and made off quickly.

In the distance one saw men walking down this sunken road, when, suddenly, there would be a shell burst, with a lot of smoke, and, when this cleared, they would have disappeared. Eventually, I reached the field hospital, where I fainted off. Later, some of us were taken to the railway station to be put on an hospital train. This was bombed on our arrival and we had to take cover. After some delay the train started off.

*   *   *   *   *

How sweet it seemed to hear the rhythmic movement of the train, putting more and more distance between us and "the hell" we had just left. All we could think of was a rest in a comfortable bed and time to forget.

I have never been able to completely do this and dream of the sunken road to this day.

Section Five
NORFOLK SOCIETIES

Main Entrance, Trinity Hospital, Castle Rising

RELIGIOUS GILDS IN NORFOLK

FIVE HUNDRED years ago, Norfolk, according to the Paston Letters, was "right wild". Though the county was outside the battle area of the Wars of the Roses, it was disturbed by private feuds of the great, violence might visit any man's threshold, and justice for humble folk was hard to come by. Many of the latter bound themselves together in religious gilds, and as early as 1381 there were more here than in any other county. These religious gilds of the villages were distinct from the trade gilds of towns, though these had their religious associations.

Why were the religious gilds so popular? Partly because the ever-present sense of danger made people crave for the moral support afforded by unity. They believed, too, that the observance of the duties imposed by the rules were preparation for entry into that other world into which they might be so suddenly precipitated. In fact, an authority suggests, membership of a gild was looked upon as "spiritual insurance".

The medieval world was reflected in religious ideas. Just as men attached themselves to some powerful lord upon earth, so the gilds were dedicated to a special saint in heaven. They were also the benefit societies of the day; any member who happened " to falle at mischief" through no fault of his own, was usually helped by a contribution from the funds. Thus, the gild of St. Christopher at Outwell, and of the Holy Trinity at Roughton, gave 7d. a week to a distressed brother or sister. Members might also borrow from the funds, the rate of interest at Little Walsingham and at Wymondham being 10 per cent. "Cristen mennes bereynge" was commonly given at the cost of the gild, if the dead brother had "nought in power of his own catelle" (possessions). A procession of the gild attended upon the body at the burial, and provision was made for the saying of masses for the soul of the dead. If a brother perished by land or by water, his corpse was sought for at varying distances. At Wiggenhall the members of St. Peter's gild were to seek "three myle about", whilst those of the Assumption and St. John the Baptist of the same place went six.

Each gild had its feast. "Every year", said the ordinance of a gild, "the members are accustomed to eat together,

147

that is because by that means greater affection can be nourished by all the members of the said gild." The feast was a symbol of unity to both Christian and Pagan. The gild feast had a spirit in common with the drinking halls of the Vikings, and the Jubilee dinners of later days. Sometimes these feasts were paid for entirely from gild funds, sometimes members made individual contributions as well— at Oxborough it was a loaf of bread. The accounts of the united gilds of Our Lady, St. George, and St. Anne at Walsingham in 1541 include payments for the following items—beef, a calf with purtenances thereof, other calves, two half sheep, a lamb, six pigs, seven rabbits, a breast of veal, eggs, butter, cream, milk, pepper, vinegar, cloves, mace, sugar, dates, and honey. The cook was paid eighteen pence, and the man who baked the pastry got four pence. Most feasts were probably not nearly so grand as this one, but no doubt the members of any gild were loath to miss the annual celebration through sickness, or other mischance. In such cases, the member was sometimes compensated from the funds, or had the right of sending another diner in his stead. Feasts were held in a hired room or special hall, if the gild was rich enough to own such a building.

The income of most gilds in the early days was meagre, the members being generally "common or middling folk". Sometimes, though rarely, the founders made grants of land; there was often an annual subscription, and occasionally an entrance fee in money or kind. The gild at Watlington charged new members four and a half bushels of barley, but generally a poor man was not debarred from joining a gild by such a formidable obstacle.

Fines in money or candle wax for breaking the rules of the gild also served to swell the funds. For the duties of a gild involved expenditure, and during the 15th and 16th centuries these funds increased. Besides the fund for needy brethren, the gild gave alms to those in want outside the fraternity. They helped to repair and ornament the parish church, sometimes having a side chapel of their own. A rich and ambitious gild might build and maintain a separate chapel, and employ a chaplain. At Thetford, the gild of Our Lady's Nativity employed three priests to celebrate in a chapel without the town, for the benefit of folk who came there upon a market day. The gilds, whether rich or poor, had their candles to keep burning before the images of their patron saints. They looked upon this as one of their foremost duties.

Not all the duties carried out by gild members were dependent on their purses. They must maintain love and

148

charity among themselves, and keep the peace. At Wymondham a brother and sister who should "hap to be wrothe together", were not allowed to go to Law until they had allowed the gild to try and settle the quarrel. One gild decreed that a brother who laid hands violently upon another was to pay two pounds of wax, besides what the Law demanded of him. Members had the duty of praying for one another, both those living and in "ye better payne of purgatore", and also for "men and all Christians". They were bound to attend the services of the church at speci- fied times, and upon the festival day they often went in procession "two and two, with slow gait". For non-attend- ance in church there was a fine payable in money or wax. Presumably people slipped out of church early upon occasions, for there was an injunction that they should stay there all the time of the service.

Although gilds were mostly composed of humble people, master and man were sometimes fellow members. Husbands and wives might belong to the same gild, and the names of single women appear upon the rolls. Most gilds admitted women to membership, generally, but not always, on equal terms with men. At Roughton the female members do not seem to have had a voice in the election of officers. This was an age when there was but little respect for the opinions of women. The right treatment for a troublesome wife is described as follows: "He smote her with his fist down to the earth. And with his foot he struck her in the visage and brake her nose, and all her life after she had her nose crooked that she might not for shame show her visage it was so foul blemished. Therefore the wife ought to suffer, and let the husband have the word and be master."

The officers of a gild were usually an alderman and a dean, though as time went on the organisation at some places became more elaborate. These officers served for a year, and were chosen by members, "for themselves from themselves".

At the dissolution of the monasteries in the reign of Henry VIII, the gilds were dissolved also. Their extinction was to be regretted; they gave joy and satisfaction to the humble, and fostered ideals of love and charity. Moreover, they afforded opportunity for self-government in an Eng- land so unlike our own—an England where men were so much more cruel and violent than they are today, but so much more artistic too. In the 14th century churches were being built in Norfolk villages; these villages were em- bowered in the wilderness of thicket and woodland, heath and turf. It was a Norfolk far more beautiful than our own, and that beauty was reflected in the arts of the people.

RELIGIOUS LIFE
IN A MARKET TOWN

MARKET TOWNS were, in the 1800s, famous for the number of public houses and churches each contained; nearly all the different denominations being represented. Later on, the Salvation Army, after a visit by General Booth, started a branch in nearly all the small towns in Norfolk. Many people were impressed by the General's straightforward preaching and became members, but, like the "Methody's" of earlier years, they were persecuted for their faith in much the same way (1783).

Here are a few extracts which appeared in an early newspaper; The *Waveney Valley Weekly News* of 1872.

"In all places where the Methodists went to preach, they met with great opposition and persecution from organised bands of hooligans.

"Numbers of the preachers were often dragged from their desks where they were 'holding forth' and rolled in the mud, pelted with rotten eggs and vegetables, smeared with all kinds of filth and drenched with water.

"On one occasion, a Mr. Thomas Lee, who came to speak to the people in the Market Place, was set upon by a gang of hooligans who proceeded to 'rough him up', whilst others rang the church bells to 'put down this preacher of sedition'. Finally, they drenched the unfortunate man with water.

"He was compelled to give over preaching and was glad to take refuge in a friend's house, while the hooligans outside kept up a continuous 'din' with a 'rough band'.*

"Mr. Lee was ultimately compelled to leave the town, in order to save the people of the house who had given him shelter, from reprisals by the hooligans.

"After Mr. Lee left the town, a 'shindy' broke out between rival gangs, but this the Parish Constables soon put down, but there is no record that these 'parish protectors' ever did anything to stop the hooligans when they were causing disorders by attacking the 'Methodys'."

*A "rough band" was composed of a number of people beating on pieces of tin or old kitchen utensils with a stick.

"Later in 1785, a Mr. Taylor, who had been 'run out of the town', by the same methods as Mr. Lee, returned. The few Methodists remaining in the town decided to stand by him and give him their support in forming a strong Methodist party, but certain dissolute citizens, hearing of his arrival, could see a direct threat to their way of life, so they arranged for a meeting at the 'King's Head' to talk the matter over and arrange for a 'proper' reception.

"As one man put it, 'Well, if this 'ere Taylor be a-comin' with his pratin', us ought ter show 'em what sort o' blood be in this 'ere town. What d'yer say to that?' This statement was loudly cheered, and a collection was started on the spot for money to buy 'ammunition' for the 'reception'— one to rid the town of these 'Methodys' for all time.

"Mr. Taylor was due to preach in the Market Place the next day, when a huge crowd gathered to 'welcome' the preacher. Jugs of ale were passed round by the landlords of the inns hard by, 'to keep up the spirits of the crowd' till Taylor should appear.

"Excitement rose higher and higher, with the crowd chanting:

'The Methodys have come to town
To try and pull the churches down'

"Taylor at last made his appearance and none would have dared, except a very courageous man, to have walked with a firm step to take up his position to speak to the people. The crowd was very threatening but Taylor, who was quite a young man, said to them:

'My good friends, why is it you wish to raise a riot? If I have injured any man tell me, if I have spoken ill of anyone here, let him stand forth. I am here on an errand of peace, not warfare. Lay down your weapons for I am unarmed and, if you will listen, I will tell you something worth the hearing.'

"For a brief space, the crowd were silent and somewhat taken aback by Taylor's fair words; there was also some hesitation by the leaders of the hooligans until the crowd were 'egged on' by the more violent elements with jeers and cries of 'you know what we're here for!'

"They rushed and bowled over the preacher and his supporters, at the same time pelting the 'Methodys' with rotten eggs and vegetables. Order was only restored when Taylor surrendered to save himself and his friends from further injury.

" 'You'll ha' ta cum along ter the Justices', roared the mob, hustling the preacher along, intending to take him to the nearest Justice, who lived at Burston. Bob Jones, lately converted, and the few that remained were powerless to protect the preacher from further violence, as the crowd now numbered over two hundred, but he knew that, if by some means the leaders could be got rid of, the mob would soon disperse and go home.

"So, during a temporary pause by the side of the road, while the leaders went to a nearby tavern to obtain more ale for the mob, Bob Jones agreed with his friends, on a certain scheme, which, if it worked, would have the desired effect of getting rid of the leaders of the mob.

"The procession moved on again, and it became darker and a drizzling rain began to fall. Several of the mob became disheartened and made for home.

*   *   *   *   *

"It was very late when they arrived at the Justice's house and the good man and his family had retired as it was his practice to keep good hours.

"Being awakened by all the shouting outside, he was not at all pleased and shouted 'What is the meaning of all this disturbance? Get about your business at once!'

"The leader of the mob replied, 'An' it please your Worship an' it's our business to bring this 'ere 'Methodys' preacher afore you, as he's bin a-prayin' and carrying on and makin' a mischief in the town and we want yer worship's advice as ter what we should do wi' him.'

" 'My advice is "Go home quietly and go to bed" ', replied the Justice and with this, fastened the window and closed the interview.

"At this unexpected rebuff, the mob became noisy and shouted: 'Take him ter the Roydon Justice' and proceeded to hustle Taylor down the drive, while the leader of the mob and a companion sought to obtain another interview with the Burston Justice without avail.

"This is where Bob Jones slipped away from the mob and disappeared into the shrubbery.

"Rain had stopped and a faint chime from the church clock proclaimed it to be eleven p.m.

" 'Did you hear that?', said the leader to his companion. 'It's just struck eleven.' But his companion was busy looking back in the direction of the beeches which surrounded the mansion they had just left. Presently he called out in a frightened voice: 'Good heavens, what's that?'

"The leader looked back and a chill of fear passed through them both as they saw a tall figure clothed in white slowly advancing in their direction. They broke down completely and, probably, for the first time in their lives, they uttered a prayer. 'Lord preserve us'.

"As the figure drew nearer, it lifted an arm and pointed towards the two, cowering on their knees, and said; 'Thou persecutors of good men, take heed and mend thy ways'.

"As they looked up, the form was disappearing amongst the trees. Too frightened to move they remained rooted to the spot, still looking in the direction of the beeches.

" 'What a fearful sight we've seen this night,' said one, and 'I thought I should have died on the spot,' said the other. Then, pulling themselves together, they made off, hurrying to catch up with the mob, who were making for Roydon."

> *"Like, he who on a lonely road,*
>   *Doth walk with fear and dread—*
> *And, having once turned round,*
>   *No more doth turn his head;*
> *Because he knows that close behind,*
>   *A fearful fiend doth tread."*

Coleridge Taylor

*   *   *   *   *

"Meanwhile, the mob had taken Taylor to Roydon and, as they were approaching the Justice's house, Bob Jones rejoined the small party of Methodists, keeping the 'ghost' secret to himself. The Justice was away from home and the mob were worn out with fatigue and disappointment and most were in favour of letting the preacher go free and at this, the rough element started a 'shindy' and many were injured.

"Just then, the leader arrived with his companion and called out, 'Hold there! Put an end to all this.' The crowd did not understand the attitude of the leader and were even more astonished when he said, 'Now, lads, look ye here, the first as lays a hand on Taylor shall feel the weight of my staff, I promise yer.' Then, turning to Taylor, he shook hands with him and asked his forgiveness. The leader also shook hands with Bob Jones, who, only a short time before his conversion, had been active in persecuting the Methodists himself. However, he had been greatly impressed by their courage and fortitude and felt theirs must be the better way.

"The leader, when he shook hands with 'Bob' did not know, and would never know, that he was shaking hands with the Burston 'Ghost'."

The idea of going to the Justice was quite a natural one, as several summonses had already been issued in various parts of the county of Norfolk against Methodist preachers, of which the following is an exact copy :

"NORFOLK"

"To all High Constables, Petty Constables and others of His Majesty's Peace Officers within the said County of Norfolk

"WHEREAS we; His Majesty's Justices of the Peace for the said County of Norfolk, having received information that several disorderly persons styling themselves Methodist preachers go about raising riots to the great damage of His Majesty's liege people and against the peace of our Lord and King.

"These are in His Majesty's name to command you and every one of you, within your respective districts, to make diligent search after the said Methodist preachers and to bring him or them before some of us, His Majesty's Justices of the Peace, to be examined according to their unlawful doings.

"Given under our hands and seals, this Twelfth day of October, 1783.

"_____

"_____"

After this, the "Methodys" were never troubled again. They increased in numbers and were greatly respected, so much so, that in the year 1790, John Wesley himself preached a sermon in Diss church, kindly lent by the rector, under the sanction of Bishop Horne.

"Mr. Wesley is a good brother," said the Bishop, "let him have the church." It is said that "high and low" crowded the service, in spite of Wesley being two hours late due to an accident on the road. In the year after Wesley's visit, Diss Circuit had 310 members. Later, there was some division amongst them, branches of Primitive Methodists and United Methodist being formed. This state of affairs went on until Methodist Union was an established fact and they are now (1971) one body.

SALVATION ARMY

THE Salvation Army is a religious organisation founded by William Booth in 1865. It had its origin in the East End of London and was originally known as the Christian Mission. Borrowing the idea of military rank and discipline, Booth selected the name "Salvation Army" himself. Their motto was "Through Blood and Fire" and indeed they passed through both in the early days of their being.

The policy of the Salvation Army was to gain the confidence of the people by intimate association with the poorest and least regarded of the population. The idea spread to foreign countries and the "Army Officers" adopted the costumes of the natives in the countries where they set up branches.

They generally concentrated on raising the moral level of the very poor, with the introduction of industrial homes, maternity homes, farms and industrial schools, also shelters, hospitals, hostels and cheap food centres. Their official newspaper, *The War Cry* was sold in large numbers all over the world; also tracts and other literature in foreign languages . . .

The chief opposition to the "Army" seemed to be from business people, property owners and brewers and publicans, who could see their businesses suffering as a result of the Army attitude to strong drink. However, quite a number of society ladies joined the organisation, renouncing all their associations to dedicate their lives to the cause of uplifting and educating the very poor and destitute. One of the most well-known is Mildred Duff; as a Captain of the Army described her to a visitor: "They do say," and she lowered her voice slowly, "that she belongs to a high family, but she's never 'high' with us—just talks to us like one of ourselves, and thinks of everything and everybody. You'll see."

"A Salvationist,"said William Booth, "had to be brave, resourceful and tactful as well as being dedicated. It was no use preaching the Gospel to hungry men and women. Feed them first and save them afterwards."

"It was noticeable that rough characters would appear as soon as the 'Army' came on the scene. Often it was just two of them—a Captain (male) who would play the concertina; and an Ensign (girl) who would sing. They attracted quite a crowd on a Sunday afternoon who would be enjoying the music, when the hooligans arrived to drown the music and singing by beating on saucepan lids and making a service impossible; on occasion, stones and broken bricks were thrown. They just had to move on, sometimes

155

taking refuge in a friend's house, where the hooligans would demonstrate outside, until someone fetched the parish constable to read the riot act.

"They tried to hire some old buildings which they could use as a headquarters, but were always refused. Owners were afraid of what the influential townspeople's attitude would be; also the damage which might be done to their property. . .

"Finally, just over the river Waveney in Suffolk, they managed to hire the schoolroom on the ground floor of an old hall, which had been split up into a number of 2-room flats, most of which were on the second floor. They seemed to flourish here and formed a band, which increased their membership substantially.

"An elderly man named Ralph, an odd person, anti-social and twice convicted—once for theft and once for setting fire to straw stacks on a farm nearby, lived in a flat above the schoolroom which the 'Army' had now occupied.

"On the day the band first played at full strength, Ralph's rage knew no bounds. There is no doubt he suffered much from this 'band' nuisance and he pounded the floor and did everything he could think of to stop the noise. The parish constable was unsympathetic, knowing his record, and the old man must have been almost out of his mind.

"At last he felt something more drastic must be tried, so he hit on the idea of taking up his carpets and making a strong liquid mixture with the contents of his cesspool and pouring it all over the floor. (One cannot help thinking that the unfortunate man must have suffered as much as the Salvationists.)

"This quite upset the programme of the brass band, also the congregation 'dwindled' as a result of the horrid, evil-smelling liquid seeping through the ceiling and dripping for long periods. And, of course, this 'amiable old gentleman' kept adding to the devilish brew. A large tarpaulin had to be constantly fastened to the ceiling to ameliorate this frightful nuisance. They *had* to report this to the parish constable.

"Ralph was convicted and found guilty of causing a public mischief and was ordered to discontinue the practice at once, and make good all damage, being heavily fined as well. The old man was furious and would sometimes appear in the doorway of the 'Army' hall and shout obscenities and general abuse at the occupants. The Salvationists, no doubt, commanded much respect by their forbearance.

Just after this incident, the old man became ill and with no-one to care for him, died after a short time.

156

"The townspeople, generally, were favourable to the Salvationists and liked to hear the band and the singing on Sunday afternoons in the Market Place. On one occasion the band was marching down Crown Street towards the Market Place and turned to go down Market Hill. The big drummer, however, was a very short man and could not see over the top of his drum, so while the band and other members of the 'Army' were marching down the Hill, the big drummer was on his way, all alone, towards the Church. Later he realised his mistake and came running back to catch up with the rest of the parade.

"Some of the converts made fools of themselves when giving their 'testimony'. One man getting up and saying, 'Once my heart was as hard as a stone, but now it's as soft as a boiled cabbage'."

"The crowd good-naturedly enjoyed these occasions which made good Sunday afternoon entertainment.

*　　*　　*　　*　　*

Here is the account of one who was present when General Booth paid his one and only visit to Diss.

"He set up a huge marquee on Hewitt's meadow. Large crowds attended and there were many converts. I can remember people going up to the penitent form with the General to the accompaniment of a blare of trumpets and beating on the drum. The old General looked like a prophet straight out of the Old Testament, preaching of eternal damnation for the wicked and the wrath to come.

"His orations were used to play on the emotions of the people, who were persuaded through fear more than anything else, to devote their future life to God's work. Many of these people had formerly been loose-living and hard-drinking and they and their families profited greatly from the change in their mode of living. They later became the hard-core of the 'Army' in the town and were respected by other members of the Community.

"The General's visit did much to advance the cause of the 'Army' in Diss and, from that time, there was much more toleration."

*　　*　　*　　*　　*

157

Today (1971) all religious bodies often join forces in religious services, as can be seen on T.V. in "Songs of Praise".

Changes are continually taking place and, who can tell, in fifty years' time the whole Church (multi-racial) may be united in one vast organisation, with all its potential for good throughout the world.

THE ODD FELLOWS IN NORFOLK

OVER two centuries ago the Odd Fellows had appeared on the national scene; by 1745 The Loyal Aristarcus Lodge met at the "Oakley Arms", Southwark, the "Globe Tavern", Hatton Gardens, or the "Boar's Head", Smithfield, as the Noble Master might direct. At the end of that century many were suppressed, for their activities were confounded with those of the Corresponding Societies, which were considered seditious, as members sympathised with the aspirations of the French revolutionaries, and studied the writings of Tom Paine. The Odd Fellows were dormant but not dead.

In the next century some members tried to put new life into the society, but at first nobody seemed interested except in convivial meetings, till the Independent Order of Odd Fellows, Manchester Union was formed. The sun of State encouragement began to shine upon friendly societies. Parish rates for those in distress were enormous, and an Act of 1819 gave encouragement to "persons desirous of making provision for themselves out of their own industry. By contributions of the savings of many persons to one common fund, the most effective provision may be made to the casualties affecting all persons".

The origin of the name Odd Fellows is obscure. "There is a sort of peculiarity in the title of Odd Fellow which may seem to imply something of buffoonery, united with thoughtless revelry to those unacquainted with the real merits of the Society", remarked someone about a lodge at King's Lynn. But whether or not the name was well chosen, the Odd Fellows prospered.

The "Traveller's Rest", the first lodge of the Manchester Union of Odd Fellows in Norwich, was founded by five wool sorters from Bradford. It met at the New Brewery Tavern in Fishergate, near to the factory where the founders worked, and the first meeting was on Boxing Day, 1835. This lodge is still in existence today. By 1857, the Odd Fellows had become an important body in the land, and in that year the Annual Movable Committee of the Manchester Union was held in Norwich for six days in June, with 110 delegates present.

Some of the rules of the Lodge of Odd Fellows which met at the "Fishmongers Arms", Fishergate, in 1862 are not without humour today. "Any brother reading newspapers or printed books, laying, or offering to lay wagers, or doing any kind of business except that of the Lodge; or any brother swearing or singing an independent song, or giving an indecent toast or sentiment, during Lodge hours shall be fined 3d. or more as the cause may deserve . . . No officer or brother is allowed to speak more than twice on one subject without the permission of the president. Any brother breaking this rule shall be fined 6d. for each offence; any brother interrupting a brother whilst he is speaking shall be fined 3d. for each offence."

Another Lodge was meeting at the "Wild Man" Tavern on St. Andrew's Hill in 1866. Contributions varied from 5s. on initiation at the age of 18, and 6d. a week subscription, to £1 at 44, and 10½d. a week subscription. A clause of the initiation declaration, which a would-be Odd Fellow had to make, was "That I have had the Small-pox, been vaccinated, that I have had the Measles, Whooping Cough". Relief to a sick brother was 10s. a week, or 5s. after a a year. "Any brother receiving such pay, having occasion to walk out for the benefit of his health, must at all times leave word at his residence where he is to be found, or fined 5s. The services of a surgeon were provided, who was paid 3s. per annum for each member.

Some of these old rules and advantages may seem quaint and meagre by the standards of today. Nevertheless, membership of the Odd Fellows Society must have given a sense of fellowship and security to thousands, and have saved many from the humiliation of resort to the cold and grudging assistance of the Poor Law.

The Friendly Societies, of which the Odd Fellows is such a notable example, were probably in their origin burial clubs, for it is significant that, since the dawn of civilisation, man has attached rites to his passing into the Unknown. In the last century black scarves and crèpe for 80 brothers, two escutcheons, a skull and crossbones, hour-glass and black cushion, were provided by a lodge upon the death of a member—gruesome regalia in keeping with the funeral fashions of the day. Also, "all brothers of the lodge shall take their turn to watch the grave, two and two, each night for 14 successive nights, in alphabetical order of their names upon the books". In 1862 a Norwich lodge paid £10 on the death of a husband and £5 for his wife.

Often in English history, the voluntary society has paved the way for State legislation, and sometimes the State has found it most convenient to work through the voluntary society. Thus, the Odd Fellows became one of the Approved Societies for administering some of the provision of the National Health and Insurance Acts of 1911-12, and this practise continued till the coming of the Welfare State.

Now, many additional advantages are provided by the Society to its members, men, women, and children, and the Independent Order of Odd Fellows, Manchester Unity, is the largest friendly society in the country.

THE ROYAL NORFOLK AGRICULTURAL ASSOCIATION— THE SHOW

THE first Norfolk Agricultural Show was held on the Norwich cricket ground "without the Ber Street Gates" in 1849, and it was spoilt by the weather. Heavy rain, and a thunderstorm in the morning, prevented the arrival of much stock; also, the judges could not inspect the animals that had come. There were horses, cattle, swine, sheep, especially the West Norfolk Southdowns, which had almost ousted the traditional Norfolk horned breed, which did so well on rough pasture. Then there was a display of new implements, but a satisfactory reaping machine had not yet been introduced; the harvest was still being cut with "scythe and sickle".

No mention has come down to us of any fashionable company on the ground; nor, indeed, is there any such allusion when the Show was at Harleston, in 1870. It was beautiful weather on that occasion. Norfolk was still in a period of prosperous high farming, and nobody was suspecting the depression which was to begin in the mid 1870's, when America would be starting to pour great quantities of corn into Britain. The meadow for the Harleston Show was a mere 10 acres; the Costessey show ground, of the present Royal Norfolk Agricultural Association, extends to over 60 acres.

Nowadays, each person at the "Show" seems to assume a "Show personality". Nobody is quite his or her usual self. In spite of his smart collar and tie, that bronze-faced man is not the same fellow who was driving the cows from the yard yesterday; his wife, in her blue-and-white silk dress, is a different woman from the one who was bustling about the farmhouse kitchen not so long ago. The leader of the big bull in the Ring is "tricolated up", as is his beast at the end of the pole, but he is not the same herdsman we see upon ordinary days. Men dressed up in St. John Ambulance and Red Cross uniforms have the appear-of minor grades of Field Marshals—yesterday some of them were mild clerks in offices. Even the elegant youth with the bowler hat and shooting stick has assumed another self for the duration of the "Show". For "Show personality" is as transient as the host of tents which will soon disappear. Only the children remain unchanged, popping here and there like dogs in a fair.

For stall-holders at the "Show", the "day-before" begins with a struggle to get too many things into too small a van, and everyone thinks that her method of packing is the best. At last the driver starts off, seated amongst a cascade of baskets. Reaching the "Show" ground there is the privilege of using the Transport Gate, and driving right up to the site. Once the goods are unloaded into the gloom of the tent, the helpers are ready to arrange things. But it is a case of too many cooks spoiling the broth, and, in the end, one person is left to do it all alone. The others go outside and look about. To-day one can do forbidden things without reproof. One can walk upon the President's Lawn, where huge hydrangeas are being planted, and covered with polythene in case of bad weather. Turnstiles are open, stalls are in a state of undress. There is an aroma of humidity and sweetness in the huge Flower Show marquees, where plants are being arranged, and water cans are lying around. Here are magnificent delphiniums, and sprays of roses, down to miniature rock-gardens and grotesque cacti. Outside are unfamiliar accents, salesmen and stockmen have come from afar, and the latter will spend the disturbed hours of the midsummer night close to their animals.

Early next morning we leave home again, chosing secluded roads to miss the traffic. At the "Show" turnstiles, sheep are divided from goats, and stall-holders and Members walk through proudly without paying. The town of tents is all ready now, and the grass streets untrampled. The sun is shining, but there are some ominous clouds about. Still, it is an ill wind that blows nobody any good, and a shower sends folk into tents, where they may be induced to buy.

The first few hours are comparatively quiet; breakfast is a long way behind, and coffee is a solace. The stall-holders talk of long-past Shows. Has the present one outgrown itself? The permanent ground at Costessey may be convenient, but was it not much pleasanter to visit a different green and wooded park each year, as in the days gone by?

The crowds begin to arrive, and red-coated bandsmen start playing in a stand nearby. The rush is on, selling is brisk, and aching legs are forgotten. There is no respite from the noise; released for lunch, one enters an inferno of din. By afternoon the stall is getting hot, and sides are unlaced to let in the air. The principal displays are on in the Ring, and the firing of guns by a military contingent startles everybody. There is a marching band, then the Parade of All Cattle tempts sellers, one after another, to hurry to the grandstand to peep into the Ring. Evening comes at last, so home again after the din of the day, and in the quiet garden the roses are in full bloom.

The second day, the "Show" ground is no longer clean and fresh as it was 24 hours ago. This is the children's day, and they want to buy something for sixpence. Three-year-olds scream, and have rides on the rocking horse. Towards evening, people are observed carrying bunches of flowers, for the produce is being sold in the horticultural marquees. It is sad to see the "Show" being dismantled, the party is over for another year.

*   *   *   *   *

It used to be the Fair but now it is the "Show" which brings people out, and, like the shrubs in the garden, it has grown far too big, but it took the "Royal" at Costessey to get Agnes down.

Agnes had been a cook all her life, but she would have made an excellent pioneer. In her bag, besides her food (they rob you at the "Show), was a pair of slush boots, a raincoat, and a piece of mackintosh to cover her hat in case of rain. However, just as the car drove into the park the sun came out, and she emerged in her Sunday best. "Now I'll leave you, and come back at 6 o'clock," Agnes said to Mrs. Jones, the stall-holder, who had brought her.

Agnes wandered about taking it all in. Why should there be a furniture stall at an agricultural show, she wondered, and that man selling metal teapots what was he here for? The crowds increased, everybody looked different to his or her every-day self—like Agnes, in fact. It was getting very hot, so Agnes sat down in the shade of a marquee, and had a drink from her flask and a sandwich. Then she went into the flower tent, casting a critical eye at the exhibits. She was a good gardener herself, and, of course, if you hadn't "narthing else to do", it might be easy enough to grow sweet peas like that, or pinks, or roses. In spite of the heat, she spent a long time in that tent, stuffing pamphlets into her bag, for it was a pity not to take something for nothing.

Out into the sunshine of high noon she went. It was all very gay, and flags fluttered from hundreds of masts. Agnes had some more to eat in a shady spot; then she

164

climbed into a seat on the far side of the Ring, and watched the Royal Horse Artillery performing in a highly dangerous, but spectacular manner. It was followed by the Parade of All Cattle. "I wouldn't like ter have the mindin' o' him," remarked a lad by her side, as a great bull passed, conducted by two men with poles. Agnes turned upon him almost ferociously. "That's them young nimble bulls what you want ter keep away from," she retorted. The lad cast Agnes a rather frightened glance.

The afternoon wore on and Agnes was feeling a bit tired, and decided to go back to Mrs. Jones's stall. She set off through the throng, but it was a muddling place, and she seemed to be getting nowhere near her destination. Suddenly, with a thrill of horror, she realised she was lost.

"Can you tell me the way to Mrs. Jones's stall?" she asked of a St. John Ambulance man. He smiled, "What's on the stall?"

"Why, baskets and all that," replied Agnes. He told her to go down the Avenue towards the President's tent. "That's near there, maybe."

By now Agnes was thoroughly alarmed. This was a crazy place. She passed some ladders pitched vertically towards the sky. "Whoever wants to use a ladder like that?" she said out loud, "That's an advert, that's all that is. Waste of money! The "Show" had lost all its glory; it seemed now like Bedlam. "Go to the W.V.S. Enquiry Tent," suggested a woman, who saw her dilemma. But where was that? A long walk brought her to the pigs' enclosure. Then she retraced her steps towards the high clock in the Ring. It was nearly 6 o'clock, and she might be left stranded 20 miles from home.

Then, when her alarm was at its height, she found the Enquiry Tent. The W.V.S. woman seemed to know all about Mrs. Jones and her baskets. "But that's no use just telling me the way, 'cause I git muddled wi' all these here places," she sobbed. Yes, she actually sobbed, and nobody had ever seen Agnes cry before. The W.V.S. woman realised that Agnes was really near the end of her tether, so she told her to get into a waiting car, and in three minutes they were at Mrs. Jones's stall. But after letting go like that, Agnes could not regain her self-possession. She just sobbed and sobbed. It needed cups of tea, and repeated assurances that she had kept no-one waiting to calm her down. And all agreed with her that the "Show", like some other things, had got far too big.

165

TRINITY HOSPITAL
CASTLE RISING

ON A Sunday morning, at Castle Rising, the Sisters of
the Trinity Hospital attend church in their distinctive dress,
which attracts more attention from visitors than even the
V.I.P.s who sometimes worship there. They wear scarlet
cloaks with the badge of the Howards, a lion rampant,
embroidered on the left breast, and black hats for great
occasions, high pointed witches' ones of the traditional
design. The cloaks date from the middle of the last century.
Before that, they wore blue livery gowns of broadcloth,
and every day they were clad in dresses of strong broadcloth or kersey, a new one being provided each year. The
colour was brown, as that was a poor person's choice. For
originally the Sisters were drawn from the respectable
destitute, widows or spinsters, of the villages of Castle
Rising, Roydon, and North Wootton. Now there are no
geographical restrictions, or class distinctions. Anybody
thinks herself lucky to get a comfortable house in the
Trinity Hospital.

The hospital forms a square of mellow brick about a
courtyard, flanked by almshouses, with an entrance porch,
in which hangs a great bell; at the opposite end is the hall,
Governess's lodgings, and behind a chapel. Over the road
is the parish church, part Norman, and near by rises the
grassy mound of the castle. Lately the Trinity Hospital
has been cast back several decades into peace, for the main
coast road which used to pass it is now a dead-end since
the making of a by-pass. "It's lovely," exclaimed the Governess, for she is spared the constant fear for the elderly
women under her charge, from summer traffic.

The almshouses are now reduced from 12 to 9, and
have been modernised. They consist of a living-room, kitchen, bath-room and W.C., except in two instances, where
a bath-room is shared. Each house contains an original
Jacobean table and chair, and three have bedsteads of the
same date. The rest of the furniture is supplied by the
inmate. Bright fires burn in the grates (7s. 6d. is given
weekly towards the cost of coal) and water is heated from
a central boiler. A Sister pointed to the garden outside her
window, "I've always wished for a plot, and now I've got

one," she said. In it were her roses, some she had grown from cuttings, and a lavender hedge.

Every year on the founder's birthday, February 24th, the community meet in the hall, in cloaks and high hats, for dinner. They sit on benches beside the refectory table. Everybody has a glass of sherry or port; the traditional fare was roast beef and plum pudding, the former roasted on the spit in the open fire-place, but now these are sometimes changed for more digestible viands. Still, it takes a bag of coal to heat the place.

On appointment, Governess and Sisters are welcomed by the Assistants (trustees) and swear "to live peacably with the other Sisters . . . and to do nothing to endamage the Hospital". Now, regulations are reduced to a minimum. The Sisters may not go beyond the village without first telling the Governess, and in summer (it is too cold in winter) they attend prayers, read by the Governess each morning in the chapel. The Governess looks after anyone who is sick, and locks and unlocks the great doors leading into the courtyard night and morning. Altogether, any local authority might be proud of these grouped homes for the elderly, which ante-dated the Welfare State by more than 300 years, having been built by Henry Howard, Earl of Northampton, about 1616.

The original qualifications for admission were: "They must be of an honest life and conversation; religious, grave, discreet; able to read if such a one be had . . . to be fifty-six years of age at least; no common beggar, harlot, scold, drunkard, haunter of taverns, inns, or ale-houses . . . to go to prayers three times every day, and to say the Lord's Prayer, the Creed, and a prayer ordered by the founder; and to go to church morning and evening every Sunday and holiday, and Wednesday and Friday." It was also laid down that anybody being "guilty of atheism, heresy, blasphemy, faction in the hospital" was to be expelled.

The duties of the Governess were "to preserve the household stuff of the hospital, to take care of the sick, to cause the gates to be shut morning and evening at due hours; to deliver out the blue gowns every Sunday and holiday, and to receive the same back again at night . . . to look to the reparations of the hospital, that not so much as one stone be missing . . . to preserve the trees; to keep the garden plot fair and handsome . . ." In 1780 the monthly allowance to each Sister was eight shillings, and the Governess twelve. Also on thirteen feast days each received eight pence and the Governess a shilling. The allowance for fuel was 25½ cwt. annually to each sister, and double that amount to the Governess.

Of course there were troubles from time to time in the community. At one period in the last century, a nurse was employed to tend the sick. Apparently she was finding this too much for her, for she shook her fist in the Governess's face, and screamed out her protest. However conditions must have been secure and sheltered within those thick walls, when the world was very hard outside. The Sisters were provided with a donkey and cart to go to King's Lynn, four and a half miles away, to provision themselves, and the "dicker shud" still remains.

Castle Rising is a mysterious place, for so much of its history is lost. The sea water deserted it centuries ago; no longer has it the distinction of being a Rotten Borough, returning two Members to Parliament, with a mayor and corporation. But Trinity Hospital stands foursquare, a refuge still in an unkind world.

Section Six
MISCELLANEOUS

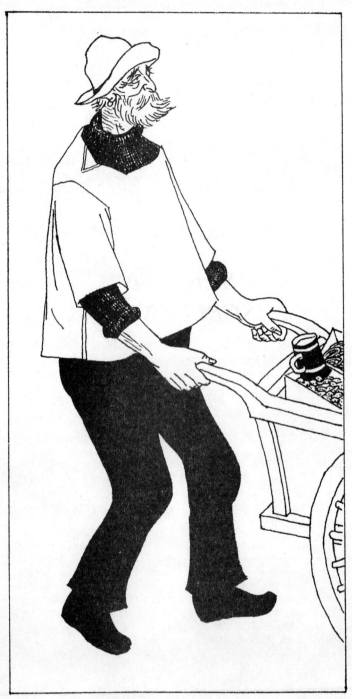

"Lovely Cockles and Winkles!"

A RAILWAY LINE THAT HAS GONE
AND ONE THAT NEVER CAME

IN AN unimaginable future, when our present day is pre-
history, it may be that the origin of both cutting and
embankment at Wells will be obscure to later men. Beneath
the bridge carrying the road near the station, the cutting,
denuded of rails, is as forlorn and lifeless as a dried-up
water course. Farther on, there are two shocking gaps,
where railway bridges have been demolished. Then the
track shoots westward over the coastal marshes, and past
the ghostly station at Holkham. Inland are the woods
about the Park; to the north, pine trees and naked sand-
hills shield the great, green plain from the sea. Beyond the
mysterious mounds and ditches of Holkham Camp, the
track swings inland, over the level crossing with its gate-
house, into a cutting pink with mallows, and over the
fields to Burnham Market, which went on receiving goods
trains from Heacham after the Wells section was closed.
Burnham station has now gone too. In the latter days of
the goods trains they behaved in a surprising fashion.
Arriving at a remote level-crossing, an engine stopped, the
driver climbed out, opened the gates, drove through, and
then had to close them again. But this line in its heyday
was the West Norfolk Junction Railway.

On a January morning in 1866, the first train to travel
along the new railway left the Heacham Junction of the
Lynn and Hunstanton line, and then proceeded as far as
Burnham Market. On board, the Deputy Chairman of the
Great Eastern Railway got more cheering than was his
due from the groups of people beside the route who mistook
him for the Prince of Wales. However, they were not to
be disappointed, for at 3 o'clock in the afternoon, the
Royal party entered a commodious saloon carriage at
Wolverton station and, a quarter of an hour later, the train
began its journey. At the Heacham junction, His Royal
Highness joined Captain Tyler, the Government Inspector,
on the engine; the train passed through Sedgeford and
Docking stations of the West Norfolk Railway, where
there was some shouting from large assemblies of spectators, and, in three-quarters of an hour, reached Burnham
Market. Here the Prince and Princess alighted, and proceeded the rest of the way to Holkham Hall by road.

171

It was not till the following August 17th, that the 18½-mile stretch of line between Heacham and Wells was opened for traffic. This delay was a disappointment to the directors, who had expected trains would be running soon after the Prince's trip. But the Board of Trade was awkward. The chairman explained that it "had insisted upon their making the same arrangements as required by the enormous traffic at Clapham Junction, which he considered superfluous on their line". The new line had been built at a cost of under £104,000, believed to be an "unprecedented economy".

There was an agreement with the Great Eastern Railway whereby that company was to manage the line, and provide rolling stock and staff for 50 per cent of the gross earnings. Considerable difference had occurred between the two companies about the payment of taxes. The Great Eastern was a growing concern which had absorbed seven East Anglian railways. Maybe the West Norfolk directors were a bit frightened of their powerful partners. At a company meeting, somebody went so far as to say, "he was glad to hear they had a good hold on the Great Eastern Railway, who, he had always considered, were slippery kind of people."

So it is a Great Eastern train that is depicted on the opening advertisement of the West Norfolk Junction Railway. The engine cuts a laughable figure to modern eyes; there are some wagons bearing private equipages, and a number of passenger coaches, with brakesman on top. His was an unenviable job in cold weather, and he was liable to become so stiff and cold that he had to be lifted off at the journey's end. A brakesman on a goods train, which was travelling down an incline, had to scramble from wagon to wagon in order to apply the brakes, a dangerous procedure, sometimes resulting in injury.

Perhaps it was just as well that the opening of the new line was delayed till after midsummer. The spring had been cold, cattle plague rife, and the depression in agriculture had affected adversely the returns of the Lynn and Hunstanton Railway. For the first five and a half years the profits of the West Norfolk Junction Railway were absorbed by a debt of £4,000 incurred over and above the original estimate, necessitated apparently by the tiresome requirements of the Government Inspector. In June, 1872 the company paid a dividend of £1.10. per cent, and by 1874 it had risen to £2.7.6. That year the West Norfolk Junction was amalgamated with the Lynn and Hunstanton Railway, which continued till 1890. Then it was taken over by the Great Eastern, which ran it for thirty-three years till it became part of the L.N.E.R. and finally of British Railways.

On the Saturday before Whitsun, 1952, the last passenger train to Wells left Heacham station, and holiday-makers had to return the following Monday by bus. Then, on January 31st the following year, the great tide swept over the deserted stretch of line across the marshes. Nature had completed its obsequies.

Now, there is no railway near the North Norfolk coast between Sheringham and King's Lynn. The miniature "Crewe" at Melton Constable, where engines were once built, is a forlorn assortment of derelict platforms and sheds. The four branch lines which radiated from here have all gone. People say it is more difficult to travel about the county in the 'seventies than it was at the beginning of the century when so many "dickey" carts were in action. However, the empty railway cuttings give pleasant shelter from the spring winds. There is a skin of turf, and early flowers bloom here in the warmth. In their latter state the tracks are sweeter than when they were tended and tarred.

*   *   *   *   *

In the latter half of the last century, when so many companies were busily scrawling the map of Norfolk with railway lines, it was only to be expected that someone would consider extending to the sea-ports of Cley and Blakeney the convenience of this iron network. The railway was so accommodating in those days! Why, the train stopped a quarter of a mile out of Holt station to enable a certain farmer to board it near his doorstep! How admirable it would be when a string of easily-moving trucks on the quays replaced the coal wagons which straining horses had to pull four or five miles, and up the hill to Holt.

The idea of a railway for Cley or Blakeney had been mooted as early as 1864. Clement Cozens-Hardy of Cley Hall wrote to his brother, "I hope you will put in a word for the Station at Cley, for there is more trade done at Cley that at Blakeney, and if there is no Station at Cley that trade would gradually depart from Cley, as merchants would naturally take up their abode at Blakeney." Some years later he wrote, "Blakeney merchants do not want the rail. They think it would injure the shipping . . . the Engineer said it would save 12 per cent if they began the line at Cley because of getting the materials by water." This last remark illustrates what an enormous change has taken place over a century in Cley's access to the sea. However, these railway projects came to nothing, but in 1884, one of the Melton Constable branch lines reached Holt.

173

In the 19th century, the trade of Blakeney was still considerable. In 1863, there arrived here 184 coasting vessels, and 14 from the Baltic and Mediterranean; outward bound ships numbered 120, and their cargoes were principally corn and malt. The harbour had been improved, and part of the channel straightened and shortened under the provisions of an Act passed earlier in the century. The extension planned when the railway reached Holt was to avoid the quay at Blakeney, which was considered too inaccessable for development. Instead, the railway was to bypass the quay and continue westward to Morston, where a line, just over a mile in length, would lead across the tidal marshes to the shores of "The Pit" in Blakeney channel, opposite the Point, and "near the low water mark of the ordinary spring tides". Here a wharf was to be built, 360 yards to the west of the junction of the Morston creek and the Blakeney channel. This wharf was to be protected by an embankment or breakwater, causing sand and mud to accumulate. This was to extend westward as far as a point in Warham All Saints, and upon it and the wharf such lights, as Trinity House should direct, were to be kept burning from sunset to sunrise. Ships would be able to unladen here in sheltered anchorage afforded by Blakeney Point, and the long and rapidly silting channels to Cley and Blakeney would not have to be used.

Plans took a long time to mature, so much so that land which had been bought for a station at Cley had been taken over by some unauthorised person who had enclosed it, and occupied it long enough to establish Squatter's Rights! A start was made on the new track, which was to leave the railway where the Holt-Cromer road crossed it, but it was soon stopped, and the idea was abandoned.

Why was this grandiose scheme allowed to perish? One legend is that a representative of the company visited Blakeney on a bitter winter's day, with the north wind sweeping across the flats left by the receding tide. He felt so cold, exposed as he was to the North Pole, and the prospect impressed him so unfavourably, that he recommended the discontinuance of the scheme. Another and more likely tale is that a director who was going to largely finance the extension died soon after it was started. So Blakeney "a very ancient harbour, and much frequented by ships and vessels of large burden . . . situated so as to afford good shelter and protection in strong westerly, northerly, and easterly winds to all vessels trading on the Norfolk coast", with Cley and Morston were left to lapse into charming old age, a refuge for the weary from the wastes of urban Britain.

DEVIL'S DYKES AND LAUNDITCH

NOBODY knew what they were there for, and the banks and ditches, if not exactly sinister, were so perplexing as to purpose, that folk took fright and called them Devil's Ditches. It was raining and the trees of the Forestry Commission were soaking wet, but the man on the bicycle dismounted when he was hailed. "Devil's Ditch, that's farther along, the road goes over it. Who made it? I don't know, that was before my time!" He smiled, the rain drops were trickling down his face. Beyond the woods, the road from Garboldisham to Thetford split the ancient ditch, which runs from the Little Ouse, northward across Garboldisham Heath to East Harling. It was filled with bracken and small trees and a solitary pine brooded over it. "I walk along there when I'm out shooting," said the farmer from Middle Farm, "nobody has ever dug down as far as I know, but the foundations of a Saxon house were found on my land not far away.

There are several Devil's Dykes or Ditches in south-west and south Norfolk, and one in the centre of the county, but this, for some unknown reason, has not been assigned to the Devil, but is called the Launditch. It was almost as mysterious 200 years ago, and the author of the note had not seen it himself, for he wrote "I am told . . . the features of the country are in some places bold and beautiful . . . the ditch from which this hundred is said to take its name (says Mr. Parkin) begins near Wendling Carr. This dyke or barrier is yet visible in many places, and was no doubt a division or boundary of lands lying on each side; but some who are fond of extraordinaries fondly magnify this simple landmark into a warlike trench." Yet according to present-day opinion the latter were right. Early in the Dark Ages, after the Romans had left Britain, the Launditch and the other dykes were made by Angles or Saxons who had come from lands over the North Sea. They were "a warlike but not a military people", and the ditches they dug out were probably both for tribal defence and marking territory. The Launditch lay athwart a Roman road running from east to west, and the name is by interpretation Lawa's Dyke.

In more spectacular parts of the county than the Launditch area the narrow side roads are quite busy on a Sunday afternoon in summer with sight-seers and drivers who ask the way, but the labyrinth of central Norfolk, between the red lines on the map, is almost deserted. It is cosy amongst the fields bursting with barley, warm and sleepy within the hedges. A man in shirt-sleeves with a bronzed face leant over his gate, the garden behind was bright with flowers and the little old house seemed to grow out of it. "Do you know where the Launditch is?" There was a momentary pause, "Never heard tell on it" was the reply. It was the same answer again and again, though somebody at Longham said "They reckon this here is a Roman rud". Bell Hall Farm off the Longham-Litcham road seemed a hopeful place for the search, though the half-inch map was no help. Bell Hall proved to be a small plain house with blue tiles; it was quiet and deserted. On the shaggy lawn were the remains of a bonfire, and a spray of rose bush and some goosegrass sprawled across the doorway. The untidy yard was nettle-grown, and through a space in the barn wall showed a bale of discoloured straw. There the visit ended for that day. Even a man in the lane who had once worked at Bell Hall said he knew nothing of the Launditch.

Still the lonely farm called, and lead to another search. One side of the lane was banked and overgrown with bushes, small trees and grass. There was a struggle to get through these obstacles, but from the adjoining field one peered into it—the Launditch. The black Labrador slipped into the dappled shade; maybe from her dog's subconscious mind she sensed forgotten men. The old defensive ditch had been put away by time, forgotten and hidden from all but prying eyes. Farther north, vestiges of the ditch can be traced to Mileham ; the southern part of the Launditch is said to begin at Wendling Carr, continues over a disused airfield, and so on to Bell Hall, which is the most spectacular stretch of it.

What most passers-by see of Wendling is not very attractive, a few scattered houses by the dark, bustling Dereham to Swaffham road. But away from the highway there are old stout cottages at peace. Carr Lane leads to a farm, and here is a long meadow with a stream and black-and-white cows. Once there was an abbey in the meadow, for the pagans of the Launditch had turned Christian, and in the 12th century came the white canons of the Premonstratensian order. This order had been founded in France by St. Norbert. The name means "the meadow pointed out" for Norbert had dreamt of the place where the first canons were to dwell. The Wendling Abbey contained what the faithful believed to be parts of the true Cross and the foot of St. Lucy the Virgin. The monastic buildings had a history of disrepair. In 1411 the Pope granted an indulgence to penitents who should give alms for repair of the canons' church. Sixty or so years later, the abbot was ordered to rebuild the church which had been burnt; the number of canons had fallen to only four besides the abbot and sub-prior Richard Fenwick ; one of the monks, was "contumacious and rebellious" and given forty days of penance and banishment to Leicester Abbey for three years. Another offender did not sing the collects properly, but refused to ask pardon. But in 1500 Bishop Redman found 6 canons and 4 novices at Wendling, and "all was delightful". Later in the century commissioners reported of the "religious persones" that "Ther name ys nott goode", but when the abbey was dissolved the ex. abbot was given a pension of 100 shillings. It is said that the stone of the abbey was used for repairing roads; nothing remains of it to-day.

So Wendling Abbey has disappeared and the greater part of the Launditch. Some people hereabouts may disregard the ancient ditch, but they cannot escape wholly from the mysterious people who made it. For in the depths of the mind lurk hopes and fears, the race memories of scores of bygone generations.

NORFOLK FOOD—
PAST AND PRESENT

THE dumpling is the most notable of Norfolk dishes. How the Norfolk housewife came to boil the first dumpling, or "swimmer", and why this admirable food is peculiar to the county, we do not know. "The inhabitants of Norfolk," wrote the author of *The English Traveller*, have long been celebrated for their healthy constitutions, which is said to be owing to their eating such vast quantities of dumplings, that the expression 'dumpling' of late has become a proverbial phrase when other people speak of a Norfolk man . . . 'tis no uncommon thing for them to take a dumpling, after it is well boiled, and, having dipped it in goose's grease, immediately to eat it, as though it was the most delicious morsel in the universe."

Though Parson Woodforde dined in Norwich "of Norfolk Dumplings and goose, a very poor dinner", he must have respected the wholesomeness of the dumpling for he gave it to his servants, lately inoculated against the smallpox. Coming much nearer to our own day, a father used to say to his large family of children, "the one of you that eats the most dumpling shall have the most roast beef afterwards".

The Norfolk dumpling should be made of bread dough containing yeast, put to rise, and then plunged into boiling water, and boiled for twenty minutes. It is eaten with gravy, and is a cheap and delicious concoction, enjoyed by most children, which should be more fashionable to-day.

Anyone digging near the North Norfolk coast is bound, sooner or later, to turn up oyster shells, and what a feast of oysters our forebears must have enjoyed! At the beginning of the present century, oyster boats were anchored in the Pit, by Blakeney Point, but the fishery ceased about that time.

Near Wells Quay is the Whelk House. Some women were standing by it, staring out over the marshes to the sea. They were waiting for "the tide to make", and for breakers to start leaping on the distant line of the bar. That was the sign for them to light the boiler fires, for soon the boats would be coming up the channel, and the whelks in them must be boiled. The boats had been far out for perhaps eight hours or so, away to sea, where land sinks below the horizon. In foggy weather, the whelk fishermen listened anxiously for sirens, for the whelk pots were laid in the track of shipping, and there was a danger of being run down. Few whelks were sold locally; then and now they are sent to Norwich, London, and the Midland towns. As the shells lie upon stalls, amid the crowded haunts of men, who thinks of how they have been snatched, at the peril of lives, from far out across the waste of waters?

Some years ago, the cockle man's bell used to sound on market days in the Norfolk market town. "Cockles big as haystacks, mussels, winkles, samphire," he sang, and went on repeating this refrain when he was alone on the road. "I can holler down any motey-car, I can," he said. He was a rosy-faced fellow, with an apt remark for everyone. Cockles are still very popular, especially "Stewkey Blues". The shells lie in pails outside cottage doors, waiting to be boiled for tea. The salt marsh plant called locally "samphire" is botanically jointed-glasswort. It is called "The poor man's asparagus", and a pickled jar of it stands in many a Norfolk pantry.

Years ago, the fish vendor used to call in a loud voice, "Fine kippered herring". They were much enjoyed by poorer people. Kippers kept well, so often a quantity would be bought to last several days. It was possible to detect a family which had eaten red herring for tea a hundred yards away!

Many farm workers and their families ate large quantities of swedes, for they were cheap, and eked out the small amount of meat which could be afforded. Swedes were boiled until soft, then served with bread, and a small piece of butter, salt and pepper added to taste. This addiction to swedes was probably the reason why Norfolk rural folk were known as "Swede Bashers".

Owing to change of taste or fashion, the Norfolk Biffin apple is now a sweetmeat of the past. Charles Dickens pictured in the green-grocer's window "Norfolk biffins, squab and swarthy, setting off the yellow of the oranges and lemons, and in the great compactness of their juicy persons, urgently entreating and beseeching to be carried away in paper bags and eaten after dinner." In October 1769, Parson Woodforde "Gathered in my keeping apples . . . seven Bushell Baskits of the old true Beefans, so peculiar to the County of Norfolk." Biffins were very hard apples, and there were at least three kinds. They were baked for a long time in a cool oven and eaten cold.

Woodforde, who never forgot to mention what he had to eat, writes of "Norfolk batter pudding and drippings. There was a Goose roasted, it being Michaelmas day", and

Norfolk turkey at Christmas. He sent some birds to friends in London. "The Turkies were much admired at Norwich. They went by Mail Coach to London this Aft."

The Fenlanders have (or had) an unusual arrangement at dinner. "There weren't narthin' wrong with the place," explained a housekeeper from High Norfolk, "that was them there apple puddins and jam rolly-pollies afore the meat I didn't seems ter fancy. Cold bacon, they eat a load o' that an' all."

What of Scoulton Pie? Until recent years, thousands of black-headed gulls nested at Scoulton Mere. "We felt glad when the 'puets' came, that meant the spring," said a Scoulton woman, who had often eaten the eggs. They were considered a delicacy boiled, better than plovers', bigger than bantams', with reddish yolks, and the whites had a blue tinge. The first clutches of eggs (three in a nest) were collected, and the owner of the Mere sent them away to friends in boxes of a dozen. Later they were sold in London. In scarce times the birds themselves went into the pot; whether eggs or fowls formed the ingredients of the famous Pie, nobody now recollects. Neither does anybody know why, in these latter years, the Laughing Gulls have forsaken Scoulton Mere.

There were special foods for high days in Norfolk. Brown and white "Buttons" (biscuits flavoured with ginger and lemon) can be bought still in a few shops at the time of Tombland Fair (Norwich) in Holy Week, but Diss Bread seems to be a thing of the past. Good Friday bread was not all eaten on the day, but kept for a year, and, mixed to a pulp in water, was considered beneficial for physical disorders. A piece of Good Friday bread put by the threshold is a defence against witches, and is sometimes resorted to even nowadays.

A rich baked custard in pastry is the proper dish for Easter Sunday. It used to be Tansy Pudding. An old recipe is as follows: "Grate ¼ pd. of Naples biscakes and 1 nutmeg into a quart of cream, then put in 14 yolks of eggs and 6 whites. Beat and strain some spinach and a little tansy and put it to the cream. Add a little salt, and sweeten to your taste, stir in a spoonful of flour. Then put a little piece of butter into a saucepan or skillet, melt it and shake it about. Set it over a gentle fire stirring till it is as thick as butter, then pour it on a dish buttered, put it in an oven, half an hour will bake it." The Rev. C. A. Johns, author of the popular botany book, *Flowers of the Field* (first edition 1853 and many since), speaks of "a nauseous dish, Tansy Pudding". The tansy may represent the bitter herbs of the Jewish Passover.

Rabbit pie was very much in demand during "Haysel" and Harvest, when rabbits were plentiful. The best parts of the rabbit, together with the meat from a hock of pork, and a few sliced potatoes, were put in a pie dish with pastry on top. The pie was placed in a warm oven and baked slowly for 2-3 hours. Broad beans were used as a vegetable with this dish, whilst they lasted.

Harvest cake was baked and, on some farms, the harvesters each received a seed cake when "all was gathered in". This may have had a pagan significance.

Perhaps, in the end, the most widely eaten Norfolk food of these days is the short-cake. It is made of pastry, rolled out and sprinkled with currants and sugar before folding; it can be seen at any meal upon the household table, and finds its way into thousands of dinner bags.

NORFOLK HUNDREDS

THE Lord of the Manor, such an important person in the past, just manages to survive in the changed atmosphere of today, but the Hundred is all but forgotten since Kelly published in 1937 a list of the thirty-three of them which existed in Norfolk. Now, only the memory of a few hundreds is preserved in the names of rural districts.

The hundred is so old that it is even uncertain to what the name refers. Maybe it was a hundred hides of land (a hide was between 60-100 acres, enough for a family to live upon), or the neighbourhood of a hundred families, or a hundred warriors. Anyhow, from the time of King Alfred, probably before, it was an important administrative area, with a court to do justice and settle affairs. A "great court" met out of doors in some distinctive spot. In South Greenhoe (now included in the Swaffham R.D.C.) at a place described two centuries ago as "green hills or tumuli on the heath between Cockley Cley and North Pickenham", and in Gallow which has been swallowed up by the Walsingham R.D.C. at a place called Longfield Stone. In the hundred and a half of Freebridge the court met at one time by a big tumulus at Flitcham, then under an oak at Gaywood, and after that by another oak at Wiggenhall St. Germans. In Forehoe they gathered at the four mysterious hills or mounds to the south of the Norwich-Hingham road, in the parish of Carleton Forehoe, and in Humbleyard at a valley in Swardeston which was called Humbleyard.

*   *   *   *   *

During the reign of Queen Elizabeth I, hundreds had stores of military equipment; Sedgeford in Smithdon had one, and Wighton in North Greenhoe. The North Erpingham hundred store contained 400 lbs. powder, 600 of match, 270 of lead, 30 shod shovels, 30 bare shovels, 9 axes, 30 baskets (for containing earth for defence) and 5 betels (big long-handled mallets). When invasion was feared from Napoleon's army, Parson Woodforde's men, Ben and Briton went to Reepham to enrol for defence, "where they stayed all day, but returned in good time this evening about 6

182

o'clock, with two black staves in their Hands, with a black lether guard for the Hand, and on the staff was painted these letters in white figures 58 59 E.H.L.A. viz. Eynesford Hundred Loyal Association".

In the eighteen 'nineties, one of the few remaining obligations of the hundred was to pay compensation to any-one within its boundaries at a loss through riotous assembly. In 1896 somebody wrote "Not long ago country folk spoke with as much pride of their hundred as they did their village."

      *   *   *   *   *

A viewer of the Norfolk hundreds about 1780 thought well of the appearance of many but not all. Of the hundred and a half of Freebridge he wrote "there are several rivulets . . . which trickle down the cheeks of this rustic vale, and unflex themselves with the sea at or near Lynn. This hundred as well as Smithdon is delightfully situated on the verge of the Lynn channel forming, with the coast of Lincolnshire, the appearance of an amphitheatre round the west of the bay. The air is healthy and pleasant in the inland parts, though frequently piercing ; but the autumnal fog or damps, which evaporate from the fenlands are aguish and otherwise unsalutary." In the south of the county, Loddon hundred "is fertile and well cultivated. Tunstead was a well-improved country, finely varigated with mild ascents and winding valleys : many handsome seats, with a proportion of woods, water and of other objects which mark the features of a beautiful country. The Ant—this considerable river is not distinguished by any name . . . therefore thought it proper to give it one, the Ant, because it rises in the village of Antingham". Happing hundred came in for slight praise—"the marshes, commons, broads, and warrens, are indeed very extensive, and very irregular in their form and uses. Villages are nearly surrounded with unprofitable and uncultivated marshes and heaths ; the eastern part of the hundred is bleak and unsalutary". Happing means "Haep's people", and from the same derivation comes Happisburgh, one of the parishes in the hundred.

When Norfolk was parcelled out into unions of parishes after the Poor Law Amendment Act of 1834 (and also at the end of the century into rural districts, etc.) although some hundred names were adopted, new ones appeared. Smallburgh was one of the interlopers, for it was but a village of the Tunstead hundred. Walsingham, another upstart, belonged to North Greenhoe, and Downham to

183

Clackclose hundred. The St. Faiths and the Aylsham unions (later joined) were made up of parishes in South Erpingham, Eynesford, and Taverham hundreds. Docking union came into being, but there had been a hundred of that name which had lapsed years before.

Some of the unions built new workhouses, often in lonely situations, where, under the decrees of the Poor Law Amendment Act, life was exceedingly unattractive One of the most dreaded privations was the separation of families into a male and female side, and the standard of feeding was supposed to be kept lower than that prevailing outside. But some unions adopted old workhouses, Houses of Industry as they were called sometimes, which had been erected long before the 1834 Act by Incorporated Hundreds. Mitford and Launditch had one at Gressenhall, which had been built in 1776 "which very laudable work had been supported by many worthy gentlemen zealous for the welfare and happiness of their fellow men. Here, instead of what a scanty pittance will bring from the market, the poor of all ages and both sexes are decently cloathed, comfortably fed, and lodged in clean apartments, their health, morals and education properly attended to, and it is their own fault if they do not enjoy the blessings of plenty and contentment". The original building, which is quite handsome and, with more modern additions, is now used as a hostel for the elderly.

*   *   *   *   *

The hundred of Forehoe had a workhouse built in the 1770's at Wicklewood. It cost £11,000 which was borrowed at 5% interest on the curious Tontine method. Each subscriber of £100 named a juvenile to succeed to his share, the last survivor getting the total sum; in 1865 there were only three left. This Wicklewood building is used now by the Regional Hospital Board.

Times carry us relentlessly to bigger and bigger units, from hundreds to unions or rural districts, and ultimately these will be much larger still. Financially, growth may be all to the good, but the individual becomes swamped in the crowd. People could feel loyal to their hundred, but few can have any real affection of a rural district, and it is safe to say none will either for the giants upon the horizon.

*   *   *   *   *

THE NORFOLK HUNDREDS

Blofield

Brothercross

Clackclose

Clavering

Depwade

Diss

Earsham

North Erpingham

South Erpingham

Eynesford

East Flegg

West Flegg

Forehoe

Freebridge Lynn

Freebridge Marshland

Gallow

North Greenhoe

South Greenhoe

Grimshoe

Guiltcross

Happing

Henstead

Holt

Humbleyard

Launditch

Loddon

Mitford

Shropham

Smithdon

Taverham

Tunstead

Walsham

Wayland

SEA-SIDE AND STREAM

THE Mun is neither a long nor distinguished stream, but once it probably supported three mills. It rises in a boggy meadow near Northrepps Rectory and, soon after, flows through the lawns and trees of Templewood. The house is low and of single storey, with pillars before it; it has been likened to an underground station or a public lavatory, nevertheless it looks quite pleasing from the road. Templewood was built by Sir Samuel Hoare, Foreign Secretary in the 'thirties, and afterwards Lord Templewood.

The Mun's course is through the Soke of Gimingham, which was an ancient jurisdictional area, covering the villages of Northrepps, Southrepps, Knapton, Trunch, Gimingham, Trimingham, Sidestrand, and Mundesley, and was held of Edward I by the peculiar tenure of a mushroom or fungus. Later, the Soke passed to the House of Lancaster. Clement Paston, one of the early and humble Pastons, had "in Paston a five score or six score acres of land, and much thereof bond-land to Gymyngham Hall, with a poor little water-mill running by the river there". A mill still stands at Gimingham, but it is driven by electricity not water nowadays. The pool supports a swan and water lillies, and on the other side of the road there are staples in the wall of the house to which horses were tied by those who brought tumbrils full of corn to be ground at the mill.

Lower down, the Mun flows below Cook's Hill, where a sanatorium was built in 1899, in a fine sheltered position. It is now a hospital, belonging to the Health Service. Finally, the Mun falls over the over-shot wheel at Mundesley, and out into the sea at low tide. A man was standing by the wheel (which is now fixed) in Mundesley street. "I've only just bought the property," he said, "but I'm going to find out all about the stream." Mundesley mill was grinding corn till about 20 years ago, though the business was small.

*   *   *   *   *

Anybody curious enough to look back on the history of Mundesley in the first half of the last century is sure to come across Mr. Francis Wheatley, Vice-Admiral of

186

the Norfolk Coast. He must have been a great man in the parish, but now his only memorial is the table-like tombstone in the churchyard on the cliff. It was high on the cliffs that Wheatley built his "handsome mansion"; to preserve it from encroachment of the sea, he erected (in 1833) at the cost of £1000 "two massive walls forming an upper and lower terrace, the latter being ninety feet above the beach, commands an extensive marine prospect." But Wheatley's walls did not stand for long, for three years later a February storm battered them down. However, he built them up again, and they lasted his lifetime. But in 1863 they were demolished a second time, though the house remained standing. On that occasion an old inhabitant of Mundesley declared he never remembered greater destruction. Houses were left hanging over the cliffs, and "massive bones of the mammoth species" were picked up in the fallen earth.

Besides his perhaps nebulous duties as Deputy Vice-Admiral, Francis Wheatley had his own vessel, and imported about 30 cargoes of coal yearly. No doubt it was unloaded by horse and wagon when the ship was left high and dry at low water. Even before his time, nearly two centuries ago, "The place supplied North Walsham and all the neighbouring country with coals, timber, etc. which is imported and corn exported, without the convenience of a haven". But in 1806 Edmund Bartel was not impressed by Mundesley, "a struggling village, little worthy of notice".

The lifeboat was stationed "at Mr. Wheatley's", and on the highest part of the cliff was a signal station for the Preventive Service, and a rocket-throwing apparatus for rescuing ship-wrecked mariners. Mundesley had 11 fishing boats for catching herrings, crabs, lobsters, etc. Francis Wheatley finished his famous local career in 1848, at the ripe old age of 78.

A less happy sojourner at Mundesley was the writer, William Cowper, who was in ill health, and suffering from melancholia, when he came here in 1795. He was taken for a long walk by the Rev. Mr. Johnson, "he said he never walked so far in his life before, and besides he carried an umbrella to keep the wind from his eyes, which laid full in our faces, and made it quite hard work for him to get along with his 'sail'. He admitted he was almost ready to sink from fatigue". Cowper died in 1800 at Dereham.

*   *   *   *   *

Mundesley doubled its population in the second half of the last century, and the coming of the railway in 1903

187

brought in more visitors. Bartel had complained that "there is one Bathing Machine. Accommodations are very confined. Four or five houses at the utmost appear at all calculated for the purpose of lodgings, and they are situated close to the side of a dusty road". Nevertheless, perhaps, after all, some of the present-day visitors would prefer to put up by the dusty road of long ago to the dark thoroughfare with its fast 20th-century traffic.

Section Seven
NORWICH

Interior of an Early Printing Office

It is interesting to note that the earliest known book to be printed is the *Diamond Lutra*, produced in China by Wang Chick in 868.

EARLY PRINTING AND
ITS IMPACT ON NORWICH

At one period in history, books and important documents and records were produced by hand in a pen-script lettering. Most of this work was performed by the monks and other men of good family and education.

The room used for this purpose was called a scriptorium and the pay of a common scribe was one half-penny a day. The parchment used was smooth on one side and rough on the other, therefore written books had to be arranged so that the two smooth and the two rough sides would face each other.

There were also strict rules which the scribes had to observe. Silence was one of them and in order that some communication might be kept up from one to another a dumb language was evolved for use in the scriptorium. Another rule was that no artificial light was allowed for fear of a fire being started.

In the course of time, a form of printing was introduced, whereby pages from a written book, were engraved on wooden blocks and reproduced on a printing press.

About this time one of the very early printers left the service of the scriptorium and set up in business as a printer and was soon producing "the printed word" at a rate unheard of by the scriptorium. Thinking he was writing all these copies by hand the rumour soon spread "that in order to turn out so many copies in such a short time, he must surely be in league with the devil, as such speed could not have been accomplished by any other means."

This rumour came to the knowledge of the Church, who promptly laid information against him on the charge of witchcraft. He was tried, but released, after he had disclosed the method by which he had produced so many copies in such a short time.

However, his joy at being acquitted was short-lived, for he found that during his absence in prison, the Ecclesiastical authorities had confiscated all his plant and belongings on the grounds "that the work he was producing at the time of his arrest, was of an heretical nature."

Thus, from this time onwards, the manuscript books became fewer and fewer, although the work of the scribes still continued ; their writings merely serving as the means of setting down the original copy for the wood-carvers to produce the page blocks, which were used for reproducing the "manuscript" books in large numbers.

* * * * *

In 1454, two printers working in Mainz in Germany, Johann Gutenburg and Peter Schoeffer, invented the art of printing from movable types, the design of the letters followed the Gothic trend and, the method was a great move forward in the speed of production, but it compared very unfavourably with a beautifully-written book of the earlier period.

Later, in 1476, the first English printer appears on the scene viz.: William Caxton, his press being set up in Westminster Abbey. It is considered by some that this is the reason why printing "chapels" of the present-day are so named. However, other reasons have been put forward in this connection. Printing increased considerably during the next eighty years, many of the larger towns, including Norwich are named in the records, including the two universities.

Printing guilds were formed and rules made for controlling its members. They were very exclusive affairs and the high premiums and entrance fees, coupled with the conditions imposed on apprentices, kept the craft under the control of men of good family and education.

The Stationers' Company also wielded a powerful influence on the craft. For instance, one of their rules was that "no person or persons could practice the noble art, except members and those who were working under licence from the government."

Later, on account of the prolific growth of printing houses in the country, this company made and issued an edict that "all provincial printing must be ended forthwith." So, it came about that eventually printing was being carried on in London and its suburbs only, with the exception of Oxford and Cambridge, who did not come under the ban.

These restrictions may account for the long break in the records of early printers in Norwich. The Star Chamber was dissolved in 1641, which freed a large number of printers from any restrictions, but expansion was slow, maybe because the population of England and Wales was only six millions and, of this number, only about 80,000 were literate; in addition there was a rule "that the number of apprentices indentured, should not exceed the number defined by the rules."

* * * * *

In the Netherlands at this time (c. 1566) there was considerable persecution of those citizens who were opposed to the doctrines of the Catholic Church, resulting in large numbers leaving the country to escape from this tyranny.

Many of the refugees came to England, embarking at Nieuport and, after a hazardous journey across the North Sea, ultimately reaching Yarmouth on the Norfolk coast. They then dispersed to various parts of the county, Norwich receiving the largest number. Because of this influx, the City became one of the largest Dutch settlements in the country.

The government realised that their wealth and skills would be a great asset and issued a decree "that the strangers should be welcomed and made comfortable ; also, they should be encouraged to practise their various skills for which every facility should be afforded."

One of the arrivals was a young man, named Antony Solempne. He brought his wife and two sons with him and, quite soon, received the Queen's permission to "excercise his craft in the City".

The records state that he was made a freeman of the city on December 11th, 1570, on condition "that he practised no trade but the art of printing and the selling of Reynsh wine."

His earliest book, called *Der Siecken Troost,* is dated 1566. This book was reputed to have been printed by him before his charter to print had been granted and, he seems to have received some protection from Queen Elizabeth I in this matter, as, shortly afterwards, he placed the royal arms and a loyal motto on some of his books, viz. : "Godt bewaer de Coninginne Elizabeth."

It is recorded that nine publications only came, for certain, from his press, and are very rare ; one called *Certayne versus Writtene by Thomas Brooke,* was in English. Another publication was *Solempne's De Ch Psalmen David,* which is printed in his native language. Both of these books are in the Bodleian Library. This edition of the Psalms was used by the Walloons in the Blackfriars Hall, at Norwich, when it served as their church. There is no reference to Solempne's Press after 1579.

*   *   *   *   *

The following is a short list of names of some Norwich Printers, contained in the records:

Edward Martin, 1646, printed a pamphlet, entitled *Nox Populi.*

Edward Giles, 1698, also printed a pamphlet by John Stackhouse.

— Burges, 1701, issued the first newspaper in Norwich called *The Norwich Post*. He died in 1706 and his widow carried on the business.

Henry Crossgrove, 1706, founded the *Norwich Gazette*. He died on September 12th, 1744.

William Chase founded *The Norwich Mercury*. He died in 1744.

Richard Bacon, 1745, then became the owner of *The Norwich Mercury*. Later, his son carried on in his stead until his death in 1844.

John Crouse took over the *Norwich Gazette* in 1761. In 1771, the paper was known as *The Norfolk Chronicle* or *Norwich Gazette*.

Luke Hansard commenced his career as a printer by being indentured to a craftsman in Norwich named Stephen White, who had a printing office at Cockey Lane. This printer promised "to instructe ye same Luke Hansard in all ye misteries of ye noble arte of printing".

He assisted John Crouse with his newspaper at the termination of his apprenticeship for a time until he decided to go to London, where he joined up as a compositor with John Hughes and ultimately became acting manager and partner in that firm. From that time he reguarly printed the *Journals of the House of Commons* until he died.

So well known was his name in connection with the printing of *The Journals* that the official reports have been known as "Hansard" until the present time (1971).

*　　*　　*　　*　　*

In the county areas, in some small towns, there were often as many as three printers to serve a population of 3,500, providing only a poor living for each, so the printer would have to carry on another trade as well, in order to make ends meet.

One town had a large steamship agency in the front shop where a large picture of an ocean liner adorned the wall of the building with the caption: "Agents for all the principal Steamship Lines". On the floor above, however, printing was carried out on a large scale. The same reception office was used for both purposes.

Many towns enjoyed having their very own newspaper, or "local rag" as it was affectionately called. The works and offices of the newspaper were often supplemented by a "General and Commercial Printing" department in addition to a "Stationery and Book Shop".

NORWICH A PORT

NORWICH a port has always been a vexed question. From the first, Yarmouth opposed the idea. The Mayor said it was pregnant with the most ruinous consequences to the navigation of the port, and the trading interest of the town and neighbourhood. In 1818 an alternative plan was suggested of avoiding Yarmouth and making a cut a mile long across the Thurlton marshes, and then via Oulton Broad and Lake Lothing to the open sea at Lowestoft.

Three years later the new Norwich and Lowestoft Navigation Company presented a prospectus in Gray's Inn Coffee House in London. Its principal object was the making of Norwich into a port for seaborne vessels of 10 ft. draught. Opposition continued—from the North Walsham and Dilham Canal, landowners near the proposed Cut, and, of course, Yarmouth, anticipating diversion of trade to Lowestoft. Nevertheless, the scheme went on, and in May 1826 a Bill was introduced into the House of Commons in order to put it into effect. The Bill was thrown out, and great was the rejoicing at Yarmouth. However, the promoters were not discouraged, and another Bill was put forward in November. Eventually it was passed on the following day, and the Norwich city bells were rung; the "Times" coach had its horses taken out, and was dragged into Norwich by an enthusiastic throng. Mr. Crisp Brown, a corn and coal merchant, was delighted, for he had been the mainspring of the scheme. There was a great bonfire in the middle of the Market Place. People were only too willing for a spree, and fed the flames with palings and anything burnable. Some were hurried to the "clink", but their companions rescued them, and threw the doors on to the fire. Probably they were but half aware what they were celebrating; had the promoters of the Company been able to foresee the future, they would have had little to exult about.

Three years later the first seaborne vessel from Norwich tied up near Carrow Bridge. She was of 120 ton burden and had taken 28 hours over the voyage. Moreover, she was "handsomely fitted up with accommodation for passengers". On September 30th, 1833, the *City of Norwich Trader*, and the *Squire of London* reached Foundry Bridge, "and rendered this date memorable in the history of the city, by its being the day on which Norwich became a port. The ships had entered the Yare by way of the New Cut," and been towed from Surlingham Reach by a steam tug, with a band playing and flags flying. Here, unfortunately, a lad was drowned. The banks from Carrow to Foundry Bridge were thronged with people, and the directors of the Norwich and Lowestoft Navigation Company had a fine dinner at the Rampant Horse Inn.

*   *   *   *   *

Mr. Crisp Brown died in 1830. "Norwich a Port" had ruined him. In 1846, there were 18 ships lying at Foundry Bridge, laden with cork, coals, etc., waiting for delivery at the new Thorpe Station. "This proves how excellent and how practical was the plan of our late fellow-citizen, Mr. Crisp Brown, and must cause universal regret that he has failed". At the end of the century, in 1896, we read that "the Wensum and Yare afford great facilities for transport. Goods are transported chiefly by river to Yarmouth and Lowestoft, and by rail to London. Norwich still had a large trade in bombazine, crêpe, gauze, etc.; also agricultural implements. There were also paper mills, tanneries, coach works, rope, brush, and artificial manure works, but the boot and shoe trade has now become one of the staple trades of the city." Nevertheless, Norwich has not become the great port dreamed of by the promoters of the Norwich and Lowestoft Navigation Company.

SILKS IN NORWICH

STRIKES are not new. More than two hundred years ago about 400 wool combers left their employment in Norwich and encamped at Rackheath, because their masters were determined to engage a journeyman who had not served a regular apprenticeship. So journeymen from Suffolk were sent to carry on the business in Norwich; the local combers met them on the road and stopped them. That year a Norwich master wrote to a customer, "We are in grete feer because that three thousand weavers be on the road to Wydam to make riot in Norwich." Some time earlier the weavers had made another "grete riot", ostensibly to destroy calicoes, which they considered harmful to the famous Norwich stuffs; they went to the length of cutting the offending material off women's backs.

Many weavers were of foreign extraction. The first batch which came were Flemings in the 12th century, some of whom settled about Worstead as well as Norwich; the second were also Flemings, for Edward III's Queen, Phillipa, persuaded "good and trew" weavers to come over in crowds. But when did they begin to make up the beautiful and esteemed silken threads? Probably about this time, for Norwich churches were accumulating a wealth of silken vestments and altar palls.

Silk was mysterious stuff. For ages it had been imported from China, but nobody knew its origin till two missionary monks brought back some silk-worm eggs in a hollow staff to eastern Europe. The silk threads were not produced in England, for although there were mulberry tree leaves for grubs to feed on, they did not thrive here.

Persecution drove other weavers to Norwich. In the reign of Elizabeth I, other "Douchemen" came here, fleeing from the cruel Duke of Alva. By 1561, it was estimated there were 4,600 Dutch in Norwich. Again, after the French King revoked the Edict of Nantes, Protestants fled to England, bringing to Norwich the arts of making silk fabrics, brocades, satins and velvets. Later, in 1695, Gaston Martineau, a surgeon from Perigord, settled in Norwich and became a weaver. Of this family sprung the distinguished Harriet Martineau, and they owned Carrow Abbey at the beginning of the last century. Another notable Norfolk family which laid the foundations of its fortunes in

197

weaving was that of Lombe. Sir John Lombe was knighted by George I, and received £14,000 from the Government for having introduced the art of making organzine silk. John Harvey was a weaver in 1695, and this family lived at Crown Point, Whitlingham, and Joseph Gurney was in the same line before his family turned to banking.

* * * * *

The famous Norwich crêpe was introduced about 1819; it was made of silk and worstead, and became very popular for dresses, the best sorts would vie with the finest silk. Eventually came Challis, "the neatest and most elegant silk and worstead article ever manufactured". It was thinner, softer, and more pliable than crêpe, and the best of it was a unique article. John Grout produced another Norwich crêpe which was embossed, and he had centres in Norwich, Great Yarmouth, North Walsham, Bungay and elsewhere. At Norwich alone, 24 men and 389 women were engaged in making fabric, 65 of them worked in the factory, but the rest at home.

The Norwich shawl, woven of spun silk, came on the market at the beginning of the last century, being made in colours and patterns. It became enormously popular, and was sold at home and abroad. Soon after this, a new process was introduced for the production of material. This was a time of very high wages for the weaver, and he and his wife might earn as much as £15 per week. The shawls were sold retail at seven or eight guineas, and a masterly specimen might fetch fifty. Such a one was made up into a counterpane for Queen Charlotte.

Improved looms were putting people out of work, and in 1827, Wymondham weavers damaged stock and destroyed £1,000 worth of silk at Ashwellthorpe. Three men were taken to Norwich Castle, and a serious riot took place, which was quelled by Lancers and Light Horse Volunteers. At the Assizes three rioters faced a probable death sentence. The defence objected that in the King's proclamation made at the time of the disturbance some words had been changed. This pretext saved the accused their necks.

Scots weavers began copying the Norwich designs. Though they did not do so very well, they injured the Norwich trade. The industry was on the decline, unemployment amongst weavers, and disputes between masters and men at the proposed reduction of wages occurred. But in 1839 there were still 4,054 looms at work. The greater part belonged to families having only one or two. But by 1860 very much of the trade had gone North, with the introduction of machines and printed materials.

Section Eight
NORFOLK

A familiar sight in the Norfolk Harvest Fields of the 1800's

A GUIDE TO PRONUNCIATION
OF NORFOLK PLACE-NAMES

MANY years ago *Punch* published some verses about Norwich:

> *Yet were the stranger's welcome cold,*
> *Should he lay stress on Mouse or hold,*
> *In reference to Mousehold . . .*

Nowadays, Muzzle is not heard very often, but the Old English word was Mus-holt, a mouse infested wood. In these latter days hereabouts, the presence of strangers, the influence of television, radio, and telephone operators, and the fact that people read names more than they hear them spoken, have all combined to change the old pronunciation of many villages and towns. In fact, Norfolk pronunciation has long been a mystery to outsiders, but, oddly enough, some of the most misleading spellings retain their ancient sound. Few make a mistake about Wymondham or Happisburgh (nautical maps print a phonetic "Hais") or Costessey, near Norwich. However, old inhabitants of Salhouse, on the other side of the city, must be turning in their graves if they can hear the modern pronunciation—Sal-house, for it should be Sullus, which comes from the Old English word for sallows or willows.

The middle part of place-names is often not sounded in Norfolk, as in Hindolvestone (Hilderston), Haveringland (Haverland), Tacolneston (Tacolston) and Coltishall (Coltshall). Near the latter village is Hautbois (Hobbies), the pronunciation of which is such a poser to strangers. In 1044, it was spelt Hobbesse, which may mean a meadow with tussocks, or a hummock, for the village stands on an elevation. Some time ago, a broadcasting company insisted upon a local speaker calling Holme, on the north-east corner of the Wash, "Home". But the Domesday Book spelling was Hulmum, and the native-born calls it that now. Parishioners pronounce Stiffkey as it is spelt, only "foreigners" say Stewkey, but the famous cockles do bear the name, Stewkey Blues. Stiffkey means stump island, island with stumps of trees. Once Coston, in the upper Yare valley was known as Cosson, and Garvestone as Garston, but these pronunciations seem to have lapsed. Cley can be Cly or Clay. Probably the latter is right, as the old inhabitants say it. As for Weybourne, a few still call it Webburn; according to the *Oxford Dictionary of English Place-Names*, it comes from weag-burna (felon's stream) and a brook falls into the sea here. Nowadays, one hears but seldom Elsham for Aylsham. For the older generation has the treasury for traditional pronunciation; tape recordings could be used in Norfolk schools before all is changed to rootless modernity.

*   *   *   *   *

It is intriguing to consider that most of our Norfolk place-names come from the dark ages, after the Roman Legions had left, and when invaders were swarming across the North Sea. "We catch glimpses of giant figures— mostly warriors at strife. But there are ploughmen too, it seems, breaking up the primeval clod, and we hear the sound of forests crashing to the axe. Around all is the lap of the waves and the cry of seamen beaching their ships." Through the study of names, experts can gain glimpses of light into this mysterious period of the ming- ling of men, when England was being born. Quite a large number of place-names show that much of Norfolk was covered with trees; thus Holt, Lingwood, Wood Dalling, etc. indicate forest, and there were clearings at Bircham and Breckles. There was open country at Blofield (from the old English blaw—bleak (exposed), meadows at Gresham and Metton, and probably wild cats at Catfield and Catton. There are few references to arable land, but there was some at Castle, South and West Acre, Wheat- acre, and rye was grown at Roydon. There were sheep at Hardwick and Shipdham, Foulden means bird-hill, cranes frequented Cranwich and Cranworth, and cuckoos Yaxham. Many place-names come from tribes, families, and per- sonal names, and Thursford from the giant or demon of a legend.

The invaders called the ancient settled inhabitants of Nor- folk, Walas or Welsh, and a very few place-names indicate where, apparently, they were allowed to stay comparatively undisturbed; Walcot means Cottage of the Welsh and Wal- ton Farm of the Welsh. There are also some names which come from a period before the invasion, as Ouse, Lynn (a pool or lake), Creake which is derived from one of the sheltering hills.

Hardly had the invaders begun to think of Norfolk as their ancestral home when they were pillaged by the Danes. The latter were known as flotmann, and they were at New- ton Flotman, and Ashmanhaugh, which means the pirate's

202

enclosure. Notably in the East and West Flegg districts, Danish names outnumber those of the Anglo-Saxons. Thorpe was Danish, and means a hamlet of a larger village, as in Burnham Thorpe, etc.

Norfolk people are said to be suspicious of strangers; at any rate some are still sensitive about the sound of their place-names. A "Brass Hat" in a smart staff car asked the way to "Faarkenham". They looked at him "comical like", as they might have regarded a village idiot. Then one of them vouchsafed the necessary information, adding, "but you can take which rud you please, 'cause none of 'em ain't mine."

PRONUNCIATION OF SOME NORFOLK PLACE-NAMES OF WHICH THE SPELLING IS MISLEADING

Note. Local pronunciation often springs from the original derivation of place-names. Mass media, telephone operators, and strangers, have been largely responsible for spreading non-traditional or mispronunciation.

Place-name	*Pronunciation*
Acle	A-cle
Ashmanaugh	Ashmanhoe
Aylmerton	Elmerton
Aylsham	Elsham (dying out)
Bawburgh	Borber
Bawdeswell	Bawdswell
Beighton	Bayton
Belaugh (near Coltishall)	Beloe (locally Beler)
Bessingham	Bezzingham
Burgh	Borough
Bylaugh (near Dereham)	Beloe
Calthorpe	Colthorpe
Caston	Cosson (dying out)
Cley	Cly or Clay (probably latter correct)
Colney	Coney
Coltishall	Coltshall
Costessey	Cossy
Deopham	Deefham
Earsham	Ersham
Elmham	Elam
Field Dalling	Field Dawling
Foulsham	Foalsham
Fransham	Franson
Fulmodeston	Fulmuston
Garboldisham	Garboldsham
Garvestone	Garstone (dying out)
Glandford	Glarndford (locally)
Guist	Guyst
Happisburgh	Hazeborough
Hautbois	Hobbies
Haveringland	Haverland
Heacham	Hecham
Hilgay	Hilgy

Hindolvestone	Hildostone (locally Hindol)
Holme	Holme—the 'l' is sounded
Honingham	Hunningham
Hoveton	Hofton
Hunstanton	Hunstan
Hunworth	Honey (locally)
Ingoldisthorpe	Ingolsthorpe
Itteringham	Ittringham
Mattishall	Mattshall
Mautby	Morby
Mousehold Heath, Norwich	Muzzle
Mundesley	Mundsley
Keswick	Kesick
Letheringsett	Letheringsett or Laringsett
Palling	Pawling
Postwick	Posick
Potter Heigham	Potter Hayham
Raveningham	Raningham
Reepham	Reefham
Rougham	Ruffham
Roughton	Rowton
Ryburgh	Ryborough
Salhouse	Sayllus
Sall	Sorl
Scoulton	Scowton
Shotesham	Shottsham
Snettisham	Snettsham
Stiffkey	Stiffkey—"Stewkey Blues" (cockles)
Stody	Study
Swardeston	Swardston
Tacolneston	Tacolston
Thwaite	Twait
Thurning	Thurning or Thirning
Tittleshall	Tittershall
Trowse	Troose
Weybourne	Webburn
Wiveton	Wiveton—locally Wifton
Wood Dalling	Wood Dawling
Worstead	Wosted
Wretham	Wret-am
Wymondham	Windham
Lowestoft (Suffolk)	Lowestoft

GLOSSARY OF SOME
NORFOLK WORDS AND PHRASES
IN COMMON USE OR IN LIVING MEMORY

"In Norfolk where the people eat the best dumplings in the world and speak the best English." George Borrow.

A bit here and there	Handy "he's a bit here and there"
Apple Jack	Apple dumpling
Backus	Building or shed in back yard
Backus-boy	Boy who does odd jobs in yard
Beck	Stream
Beetle	Heavy wooden mallet
Betsy	Tea-kettle
Bigoty	Self-opinionated
Bloughed-up	Blocked
Bishee-barnabee	Ladybird
Bishimeer (or pishimeer)	Ant
Bolder	Real bullrush
Bor	You—as in "come along bor"
Brash or brasy	Land overgrown with rushes
Bron-i-cal	Prone to bronchitis
Brotches	Split hazel stakes for thatching
Brumbles	Brambles
Buskins	Gaiters or leggings
Capper	Go left (to a horse)
Carnser	Causeway
Carr	Low copse
Cedar	Pencil
Chalder	A large number—"a rare chalder of wild fowl"
Champ	Push food around the plate without eating (see pingle)
Clung	Juiceless, poor fruit
Cocks	Bigger sugar-beet seedlings
Colt	Young reeds
Cooshies	Sweets, especially bullseyes
Cop	To throw gently (see hull)
Copper-Jack	Odd-job boy
Crimbling	Creep about privily
Crome	Long-handled tool for clearing brambles and ditches

Crowd	Push along
Cumhether	Go right (to a horse)
Dag	Very heavy mist
Dawg	Dog
Deeke	Bank
Deen	Slightest sound
Dickey	Donkey
Dilly-cart	Fish box on wheels
Ding	A blow
Dingle	Opposite to make haste
Dingling about	Moving slowly and awkwardly
Do	Used instead of "if", "through", "otherwise"
Dodman	Snail
Dollop	Small quantity
"Don't git no farther than Wednesday"	A stupid person
Doss	Hassock
Dow	Dove, pigeon
Draw-water	Goldfinch
Drift or driftway	Lane
Dudder	Shake, tremble
Duller	An unwanted noise
Duzzy fule	Silly chump
Dwile	Floor cloth
Dydler	Dredger
Early peep	Twitch grass
Enow	Enough
Erriwiggle	Earwig
Eye of the wind	Wind blowing with tide
Fare	Intend or seem
Fare-ye-well	Goodbye
Fie	Clean out
Flag	Turf, peat
Fleet	Shallow
Fligger	Fidget
Foosey	Vegetable which has gone bad inside
Forgive	Thaw, "that forgive a bit"
Foreigner	Stranger from out of Norfolk
Fourses	Meal in harvest field at 4 p.m.
Frail	Straw basket
Frimmocking	Giving one's self airs
Frumple	Rumple
Fulfer	Mistle thrush
Furrer bushes	Furze, gorse

207

Gainer	Better method, handy
(Ungainer)	(Awkwardly placed)
Garp	Stare
Gather	Become inflamed
Gays	Pictures, "She only read the gays"
Gay cards	Picture cards in pack
Gay pony	Pony with contrasting colours
Giffle	Restless
Gobs	Lumps of fat
Gotch	Large jug of rough earthenware
Go-to-meeting clothes	Best or Sunday clothes
Groundsels	Foundations
Happened acrost	Found after a long time
Harnser	Heron
Hay	Have
Hay-Jack	Whitethroat
Haysel	Hay-harvest
Heater	Where two roads meet at an acute angle
Heater-piece	Piece of land between two acute angles
Heighn	Heighten
Herititory	Hereditory
High-geranium	Hydrangea
Highlows	Heavy lace-up boots or shoes
Hilda	Wild elder
Hin (or Hean)	Hen
Hodmadod	Snail
Holl	Wide ditch of water
Hovers	Floating vegetation
How are you a-bringing on 'em in?	How's everything?
Howdgee	"Hold-ye!" Call of boy on horse to men on top of loaded wagon
Huddren	Large and unwieldly
Huh	Aslant, "on the huh"
Hull	Throw with intent (see cop)
Hulver	Holly
Hutkin	Finger-stall
If his brains were dynamite they wouldn't blow his cap off	Foolish person
Imitate	Attempt
Ivory	Ivy
Jampt	Trod on
Jannocks	Good, new, excellent
Jiffling	Fidgeting
Keeping-room	Living-room

208

Kinder	Kind of
King George	Peacock butterfly
Koished	Thrashed
Lamper along	Take big strides
Lig	Bring along heavy load
Ligger	Lever to lift heavy weights
Ligger	Eel line suspended from a bit of wood
Lodder	Heart-shaped turf lifter
Loke	Lane
Lows	Low lying ground, boggy place
Make spare when there's plenty	Save for a rainy day
Mardle	Gossip
Mash	Marsh
Maur	Underdone
Mawkin	Scare-crow
Mawther	Young woman (in address becomes "maw")
Merriemills	Sandhills
Million	Pumpkin
Mine	My house etc.; Similarly, "yours", etc.—much used
Mock	Sow seeds alternately, not in line, "Mock 'em in"
Morth	Moth
Mucky	Undistinguished. Derogatory sense
Mulfer	Chamois leather purse drawn up with a cord
Musheroom	Mushroom
Nexter-morn	Morning of following day
Not a sight	Not up to much
Nothing only the eye-sight	Pretty scene, but of no material value. Flowers, etc. as distinct from vegetables
Pample	Tread about on one spot
Par-yard	Cow or bullock yard
Ped	Wicker container for transporting fowls
Perk	Perch (for a bird)
Perk-up	Get better, cheer up, as after an illness
Pick-cheese	Blue tit and common mallow flower
Pightle	Small field enclosed by a hedge
Pingle	Eat slowly without relish
Pit or pit-hole	Pond
Plantain	Plantation
Plunkett-hole	Depression into which springs drain
Poke	Sack or bag
Prating	Noise hens make after laying
Pricking	Spearing dabs, eels, etc.
Prongs	Forks for eating with

Pulk or pulk-hole	Small hole in marshy ground
Push	A boil
Quackle	Choke
Quant	Long pole for moving wherry along
Quicks	Live roots of grass, etc. "burning the quicks"
Quince	Thicket of gorse or furze
Raffler	Raffle
Rands or ronds	Reed-covered banks
Rape-hook	Sharpened sickle
Rattick	Noise
Rig or split	Space between furrows
Right side	Put right, "I'll soon right side him"
Ring-dow	Wood pigeon
Rip and tear	Rush about destructively
Rogerblast	Sudden wind, a whirlwind
Rokey	Foggy
Rounding	Spawning
Rub	Stone for sharpening tools
Rubbidge	Rubbish
Rud	Road
Rumbustious	Rank or coarse growth, boisterous behaviour
Sally	Female hare
Saveril	Quite a number of people or things
Scald	Highest part of a field
Scolder	Collection of, "rare scolder of folks"
Scuppet	Scoop used in mill
Seat	Sitting of eggs
Sele-of-the-day	Greeting
Sheers (the)	Counties to west and north of Norfolk
Shiver	Splinter
Shook the bitterest	In floods of tears
Short as a pie crust	Out of temper
Show corant	Ribes
Show peas	Sweet peas
Shud	Shed
Shutting-in-time	Fall of darkness
Sibits	Banns of marriage
Skep	Basket, wider at top
Skutes	Shortening lines when ploughing or planting "That go skuting away to a point"
Slade	Oozy ground
Slanterdiculer	Off the vertical
Slaver	Squit, nonsense
Smur	Heavy drizzle ,"smurring with rain"
Snachet	Clever thing

Sosh, on the sosh	On the slant, not horizontal
Soshums	Diagonally
Sour as a wedge	In a bad mood
Sow	Wood-louse
Spreed	Spread
Spoult	Brittle
Staithe	Landing stage
Stupid-upright	Just off vertical
Sunkets	Dainty bits
Teetamatorta	See-saw
Tempest	Thunder storm
Thas a-gettin' out	Weather improving
That	Used generally instead of "which or it"
That time o'day	In those days
Throngy	Hot and humid
Tide's making	Tide coming in
Time	See footnote*
Ting	To ring a small bell or beat on a tin tray to attract a swarm of bees
Tissicken	An irritating cough
Titty-totty	Very small
Together	Both, all, as in "How are you together?"
Took queer	Became ill, "turned up queer and took and died"
Tricolate up	Trim up
Troshing	Threshing
Trow	Trough
T' year	This year
Tumbler	Tumbrel
Wamble	Saunter
Wheatsel	Wheat drilling
Wherry	Vessel for cargo carrying; sail on rivers
Woosh	Go right (to a horse)
Yest	Yeast
Yorkers	Bits of string or binder twine to tie round the trousers

* Times recalled according to agricultural season—"Four years ago come next muck-spreeding", etc.

INTRODUCTION TO
Indications of Spring

ROBERT MARSHAM
OF STRATTON STRAWLESS 1709-1797

HIS passion for nature and the growing of trees began as a boy. At the age of 12 he planted an acorn, and measured the oak which sprang from it 70 years later, when it had attained large circumference. He used to have the trunks of his trees scrubbed with soap and water, and declared from experiment that specimens so treated increased in girth twice as much as those unwashed. Seven years before his death, Robert Marsham read Gilbert White's new book, *The Natural History and Antiquities of Selborne,* and this resulted in an enthusiastic correspondence between the two naturalists.

Robert Marsham did not build a new house at Stratton Strawless being more interested in trees than bricks and mortar. His son erected the present building with the white columns before it.

	Snow Drop appears. YEARS		The Thrush Sings YEARS		Hawthorn Leaf. YEARS	
Earliest	1778	Dec. 24	1735	Dec. 4	1759	Feb. 11
Latest	1795	Feb. 10	1766	Feb. 13	1784	April 22
Greatest difference	Observed in 55 years	48 days	Observed in 56 years	81 days	Observed in 59 years	70 days
Medium Time	1750	Jan. 15	1747	Jan. 14	1758	March 19

	Oak Leaf. YEARS.		Beech Leaf. YEARS		Horse Chesnut Leaf. YEARS	
Earliest	1750	March 31	1779	April 5	1763	March 10
Latest	1799	May 20	1771	May 10	1771	May 2
Greatest difference	Observed in 54 years	50 days	Observed in 53 years	35 days	Observed in 47 years	52 days
Medium Time	1757	April 26	1785	April 23	1784	April 23

	Swallows appear. YEARS		Cuckoo Sings. YEARS		Nightingale Sings YEARS	
Earliest	1736	March 30	1752	April 9	1752	April 7
Latest	1797	April 26	1767	May 7	1792	May 19
Greatest difference	Observed in 62 years	27 days	Observed in 51 years	29 days	Observed in 59 years	42 days
Medium Time	1777	April 13	1789	April 23	1784	April 28

Facsimile of page
from "The Norfolk Tour" 1829

	Birch Leaf. YEARS	Elm Leaf. YEARS	Mountain Ash Leaf. YEARS
Earliest	1750 Feb. 21	1779 March 4	1779 March 5
Latest	1771 May 4	1784 May 6	1771 May 2
Greatest difference	Observed in 52 years 72 days	Observed in 47 years 63 days	Observed in 43 years 57 days
Medium Time	1745 March 29	1773 April 6	1773 April 6

	Ring Doves Coo. YEARS	Rooks Build. YEARS	Young Rooks. YEARS
Earliest	1751 Dec. 27	1800 Feb. 2	1747 March 26
Latest	1761 March 20	1757 March 14	1766 April 24
Greatest difference	Observed in 47 years 83 days	Observed in 53 years 40 days	Observed in 52 years 29 days
Medium Time	1750 Jan. 22	1744 Feb. 21	1789 April 14

	Lime Leaf. YEARS	Maple Leaf. YEARS	Wood Anemone Blows. YEARS
Earliest	1794 March 19	1794 March 15	1790 March 16
Latest	1756 May 7	1771 May 7	1784 April 22
Greatest difference	Observed in 43 years 49 days	Observed in 34 years 53 days	Observed in 30 years 37 days
Medium Time	1796 April 13	1788 April 12	1778 April 5

Facsimile of page
from "The Norfolk Tour," 1829

	Hawthorn flowers YEARS		Frogs and Toads Croak. YEARS		Sycamore Leaf. YEARS	
Earliest	1750	April 13	1750	Feb. 20	1750	Feb. 22
Latest	1799	June 2	1771	May 4	1771	May 4
Greatest difference	Observed in 59 years	50 days	Observed in 57 years	73 days	Observed in 57 years	71 days
Medium Time	1744	May 12	1763	March 30	1744	March 30

	Chesnut Leaf. YEARS		Hornbeam Leaf. YEARS		Ash Leaf. YEARS	
Earliest	1794	March 28	1794	March 7	1779	April 2
Latest	1770	May 12	1771	May 7	1772	May 26
Greatest difference	Observed in 36 years	45 days	Observed in 40 years	61 days	Observed in 36 years	54 days
Medium Time	1776	April 21	1789	April 9	1787	April 29

	Churn Owl Sings. YEARS		Yellow Butterfly appears. YEARS		Turnip Flowers. YEARS	
Earliest	1781	April 29	1790	Jan. 10	1796	Jan. 10
Latest	1792	June 26	1783	April 17	1790	June 18
Greatest difference	Observed in 46 years	53 days	Observed in 36 years	93 days	Observed in 55 years	129 days
Medium Time	1760	May 29	1773	March 3	1742	April 15

Facsimile of Page
from "The Norfolk Tour." 1829

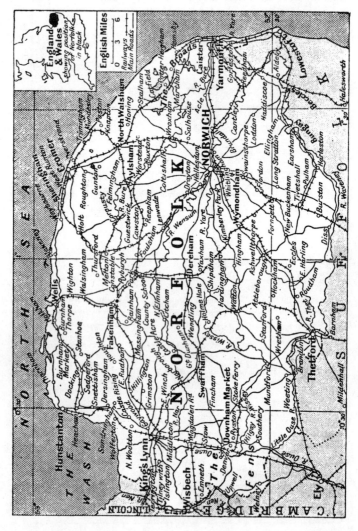

NORFOLK— Principal Railways, Rivers and Roads